$5.00

W9-BYX-746

How to Make
Soft Jewelry

Other books available from Chilton:

Robbie Fanning, Series Editor

Contemporary Quilting Series

Fast Patch: A Treasury of Strip-Quilt Projects, by Anita Hallock

Fourteen Easy Baby Quilts, by Margaret Dittman

Machine-Quilted Jackets, Vests, and Coats, by Nancy Moore

Putting on the Glitz, by Anne Boyce and Sandra L. Hatch

The Quilter's Guide to Rotary Cutting, by Donna Poster

Speed-Cut Quilts, by Donna Poster

Creative Machine Arts Series

The Button Lover's Book, by Marilyn Green

Claire Shaeffer's Fabric Sewing Guide

The Complete Book of Machine Embroidery, by Robbie and Tony Fanning

Creative Nurseries Illustrated, by Debra Terry and Juli Plooster

Creative Serging Illustrated, by Pati Palmer, Gail Brown, and Sue Green

Distinctive Serger Gifts and Crafts, by Naomi Baker and Tammy Young

The Expectant Mother's Wardrobe Planner, by Rebecca Dumlao

The Fabric Lover's Scrapbook, by Margaret Dittman

Friendship Quilts by Hand and Machine, by Carolyn Vosburg Hall

Innovative Sewing, by Gail Brown and Tammy Young

Innovative Serging, by Gail Brown and Tammy Young

Owner's Guide to Sewing Machines, Sergers, and Knitting Machines, by Gale Grigg Hazen

Petite Pizzazz, by Barb Griffin

Sew, Serge, Press, by Jan Saunders

Sewing and Collecting Vintage Fashions, by Eileen MacIntosh

Simply Serge Any Fabric, by Naomi Baker and Tammy Young

Twenty Easy Machine-Made Rugs, by Jackie Dodson

Know Your Sewing Machine Series, by Jackie Dodson

Know Your Bernina, second edition

Know Your Brother, with Jane Warnick

Know Your Elna, with Carol Ahles

Know Your New Home, with Judi Cull and Vicki Lyn Hastings

Know Your Pfaff, with Audrey Griese

Know Your Sewing Machine

Know Your Singer

Know Your Viking, with Jan Saunders

Know Your Serger Series, by Tammy Young and Naomi Baker

Know Your baby lock

Know Your Pfaff Hobbylock

Know Your White Superlock

Teach Yourself to Sew Better Series, by Jan Saunders

A Step-by-Step Guide to Your Bernina

A Step-by-Step Guide to Your New Home

A Step-by-Step Guide to Your Sewing Machine

A Step-by-Step Guide to Your Viking

How to Make
Soft Jewelry

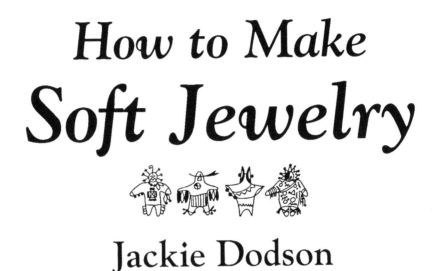

Jackie Dodson

Chilton Book Company
Radnor, Pennsylvania

Acknowledgements

Thank you:

To dj Bennett, Sherry Boemmel, Lois Christensen, Joy Clucas, Jane Elkins, Jackie Fisher, Audrey Griese, Carol Laureys, Judi Maddigan, Judy Mayo, Janna St. James Prigge, Jan Saunders, and Jane Warnick for sharing ideas and jewelry with me.

To Marilyn Tisol, a special friend, critic, and sounding-board, who made jewelry with and for me.

To Bernina of America—and Joanne Pugh in particular— for their help, and to Cheryl Robinson and baby lock for their assistance and help in answering my serging questions.

And especially to Robbie Fanning for her optimism, encouragement, and endless support.

Copyright ©1991 by Jackie Dodson

All Rights Reserved

Published in Radnor, Pennsylvania 19089, by Chilton Book Company

No part of this book may be reproduced, transmitted or stored in any form or by any means, electronic or mechanical, without prior written permission from the publisher

Designed by Martha Vercoutere

Illustrations by Jackie Dodson

Interior color photographed by Lee Lindeman and styled by Roz Carson

Manufactured in the United States of America

Library of Congress Cataloging in Publication Data

Dodson, Jackie
    How to make soft jewelry/
    Jackie Dodson.
        p. cm. —(Creative machine arts)
    Includes bibliographical references
    and index.
1. Jewelry making. 2. Textile crafts.
I. Title. II. Series.
TT212.D63 1991   91-53043
745.594'2—dc20   CIP
ISBN 0-8019-8199-9 —
ISBN 0-8019-8129-8 (pbk.)

    2 3 4 5 6 7 8 9 0 9 8 7 6 5 4 3 2

The following products that appear in this book are copyrighted or trademarked:

527, Magic Tape, Fray Check, Fasturn, Scotchgard, Goop, Glue 'n' Wash, Craft Beader, Velcro, Sculpey III, Ultrasuede, Fimo, Cernit, Fabric Cord, E-6000

Contents

Foreword

Especially as I age, one of my favorite quotes is from Vladimir Nabokov: "In a sense we are all crashing to our deaths from the top story of our birth to the flat stones of the churchyard and wondering with an immortal Alice in Wonderland at the patterns of the passing wall... Caress the details."

I sometimes feel Jackie and her world caress more details than me and mine.

We run through cats and other pets as if they were disposable diapers. Her pets seem to last for eternity. The Dodsons had a wire-haired dachshund named Otto, now gone. Jackie reports in Chapter 5 that a tiny drawn Otto appeared, like a signature, on every school paper son Steve handed in as he grew up—and now granddaughter Julie is doing the same.

We pack fifteen books, a coffeemaker, and my journal for vacation. With jewelry supplies in tow, Jackie and friend Marilyn bake Sculpey beads, wind room-length monk's cord, ransack thrift stores, and tear apart finds into funny or dazzling new creations.

We give old clothes and such to Goodwill. Jackie knows how to use every little scrap of fabric left in the universe, refashioned in descending order of magnitude: tents, quilts, clothes, rugs, necklaces, doll pins, earrings.

This is why I love Jackie Dodson's books so much. Like fully developed characters in a novel, they have a roundedness to them, which comes from years of caressing the details.

I hope you enjoy the pattern of her latest creation.

Robbie Fanning
Series Editor

 Introduction

Recently I read that a man was arrested for wearing a hummingbird around his neck. Talk about soft jewelry! He'd probably been reading fashion magazines. If you only look at the pictures, you'll see that this is the Jewelry Age and anything goes—well, almost anything.

Often not "good" jewelry, soft jewelry is everything from whimsical or silly to traditional and lovely. It isn't what I'd call "costume" jewelry either, because I think of costume jewelry as "fake" disguised as "good." Instead, jewelry today is original and doesn't imitate anything. It's often handmade from inexpensive ingredients such as oven-baked clay, plastic, or strung-together trinkets. Sometimes it is made with painting or embroidery on fabric from silk to muslin.

When I started making soft jewelry several years ago, I looked for a source book I could refer to. Craft stores offered jewelry booklets, but nowhere could I find one book with all the directions I needed for varieties of cords; how to make, string, and apply beads; and how to knot or sew closures. I also wanted ideas I could use for jewelry to make in a minute or make for an heirloom. When I didn't find it, this book of handmade, soft jewelry was born.

Soft jewelry making is a perfect medium for pack rats, and do I ever qualify! I have antique buttons, braids, beads, lace, fabric, and ribbon from two grandmothers, my mother (and all her friends), and dozens of house sales,

auctions, and thrift shops. I buy beaded necklaces to take apart and make other necklaces, and when I see interesting yarn, I buy it to put away for an idea I'll have in the future. I'm the one who buys the tumbled stones, leather scraps, and tangled threads at garage sales, and I use my vast collection to decorate doll pins, make pendants, sew on earrings, and I don't know what—yet.

Each project in this book begins with a list of the supplies you'll need. Look around you. You probably have jewelry supplies in your sewing room, the kitchen cabinet, toy box, basement workshop, even the fishing tackle box.

Along with directions for making cords, beads, and closures, I'll show you how to use them when putting together necklaces, pins, earrings, barrettes, shoe clips, and bracelets. These are jewelry projects to make for and with your children, sell at craft shows, use in sewing classes, make for gifts, for holidays, for dress up, for fun.

You'll find dozens of instant ideas sprinkled throughout the book—sometimes only an illustration or a sentence. That's often enough to get you started creating soft jewelry.

I've included not only my jewelry, but that of friends and other fiber artists, who shared ideas and inspired me. Now I have the reference book I've been looking for—and I didn't need a single hummingbird.

Cross Index

Introduction

Use this section when looking for particular jewelry you want to make or a technique you want to learn.

And if you need jewelry in a hurry for a gift, bazaar, or for yourself, check "Instant Ideas" found at the end of each heading. You can quickly look up ideas that can be just as quickly accomplished.

1. Getting Started

Each idea in this book can start you thinking of dozens more, so keep a notebook handy to record and sketch your inspirations.

No matter what kind of soft necklace you want to make in the future, you can refer back to the cords found here for one that will suit you. Use them individually or combine some or all of them for your necklaces, bracelets, even pins and earrings.

Although not always soft, you have to think beads, too, in a book of jewelry. I've devoted a chapter to beads, including those you can buy at craft stores or mail order (see Sources of Supplies); but wait until you make your own beads—you'll have the best time! I've included jewelry made with each kind of bead and cord I've described.

Another chapter teaches you how to hold everything together when you learn to attach closures.

The right tool makes the job easier. I've compiled a list of all the tools and supplies I used when making the jewelry in this book. Look through the list. You probably have many of the supplies already.

Supplies

1. Water-erasable and vanishing markers for light fabrics; white opaque markers for drawing on water-soluble stabilizer; white chalk pencil for marking dark fabric and suede; fine, black permanent marker (all available at fabric stores and sometimes craft and quilt shops).

2. 6" x 24" (15cm x 61cm) clear, plastic ruler; and 12" (31cm) clear rulers with grid marks are also helpful.

3. Rotary cutting wheel, circle cutter, and mat (grid marked in 1" [2.5cm] squares and a bias), curved scissors, embroidery scissors, fabric shears, paper-cutting scissors

1.1 Rotary cutter

4. Sewing machine (with decorative stitches) and serger

5. Knitting machine, two double-pointed knitting needles, spool with four nails

6. Presser feet:

a. zipper foot

b. cording foot

c. open embroidery foot

d. general purpose (zigzag)

e. Bernina's knitter's or bulky overlock foot (fits Berninas only)

f. Elna's net curtain or no-snag foot, which is adaptable for any machine with the use of an adaptor shank. The foot is used for sewing looped surfaces and looks like an open embroidery foot with a bar across the end of the toes to keep the fabric loops from becoming entangled.

g. It's possible to make your no-snag foot by wrapping the toes of an embroidery foot with Magic Tape.

7. Beading needle assortments, hand-sewing needle, crewel needle, doll needle, darning needle, sewing machine needle assortment

Beading needles come in several diameters or

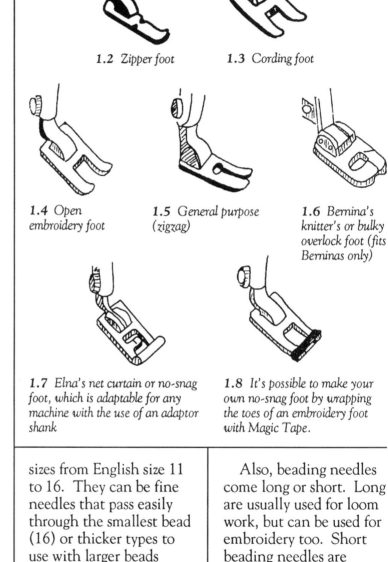

1.2 Zipper foot

1.3 Cording foot

1.4 Open embroidery foot

1.5 General purpose (zigzag)

1.6 Bernina's knitter's or bulky overlock foot (fits Berninas only)

1.7 Elna's net curtain or no-snag foot, which is adaptable for any machine with the use of an adaptor shank

1.8 It's possible to make your own no-snag foot by wrapping the toes of an embroidery foot with Magic Tape.

sizes from English size 11 to 16. They can be fine needles that pass easily through the smallest bead (16) or thicker types to use with larger beads (11). Match needles to beads, then choose thread that will slip into the needle eyes.

Also, beading needles come long or short. Long are usually used for loom work, but can be used for embroidery too. Short beading needles are usually used for embroidery, but it is up to one's own preference.

8. Polyester sewing threads, monofilament nylon thread, gimp, rayon machine-embroidery threads, gold metallic threads, ribbon floss and braids, thick metallics for bobbin and serger looper, beading thread, waxed linen thread, round leather lacing, 6-lb.-test fishing line

9. Decorative yarns, double-faced satin ribbon, muslin-covered cord, cable cord

10. Glitzy knits; silk; velveteen; Ultrasuede; Facile; chamois; furs; muslin; taffeta, silky and other dress fabrics

11. Fringe forks come in various sizes. You'll need one for the boas (see Color Plates 2 and 13). Buy them or make your own. To make a fringe fork, first decide how high you want the fringe. Double the height of the fringe plus 1/4" (6mm). For example, for fringe 2" (5cm) high, make the fringe fork twice this, or 4" (10cm) plus 1/4" (6.4mm) or 4-1/4" (11cm) wide. When stitching down the center of the fringe fork, I use a medium-wide, short-

length zigzag stitch, usually stitch width 3, stitch length 1, and a closed toe presser foot to keep the cords from tangling in it. A general purpose foot works, but it takes much more time to hold the yarn flat to the bed of the machine as you stitch over it.

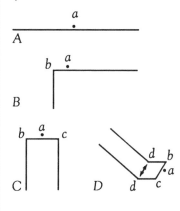

1.9 *Fringe fork*
A. Straighten heavy wire and mark mid-point (a)
B. Bend wire at a 90-degree angle 1" (2.5cm) from midpoint (b).
C. Repeat at other side of mid-point (c).
D. Bend up from 1-1/2" (4cm) to make winding yarn easier (d).

12. Adding machine tape (is used with a fringe fork for sewing long strips of fabric so they don't twist), water-soluble stabilizer, tear-away stabilizer, freezer paper

13. Bonded batting and fiberfill

14. Fray Check keeps edges from raveling.

15. Fasturn tube turners help you turn the finest spaghetti straps with no problem (see Sources of Supplies).

16. Glues and adhesives: Both E-6000 jewelry adhesive and 527 jewelry cement are available at bead shops, some craft stores, or see Sources of Supplies. Household Goop is an adhesive like E-6000 and it's available at the hardware store (I use it whenever possible). Glue 'n' Wash; glue sticks; 527 jewelry cement; cyranoacrylate (Krazy, Super, Epoxy) glues; white craft glue; tacky glue (thick craft glue) (all are available at craft, fabric, and sometimes variety and hardware stores)

17. Needle-nosed pliers, leather punch sets and heavy cardboard, hemostat, wire cutter

1.10 Needle-nosed pliers

1.11 Leather punch

1.12 Hemostat

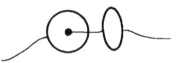

1.13 Wire cutter

18. Craft Beader set or toothpicks

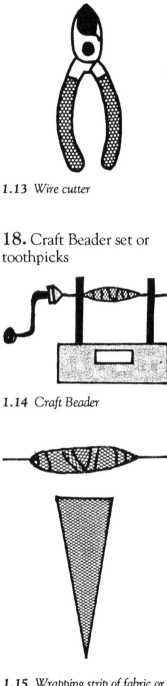

1.14 Craft Beader

1.15 Wrapping strip of fabric or paper on toothpick

19. Velcro dots, large snaps, large hooks

20. Bead assortment (I've used rondelles, pony beads, seed beads, bugles, macramé beads, as well as odd beads from broken necklaces); worry dolls; feathers; trinkets; buttons; found objects; porcupine quills; swivels; bangles; bells

1.16 Rondelles

1.17 Pony beads

1.18 Seed beads

1.19 Bugles

1.20 Macramé bead

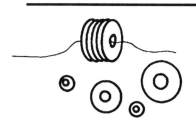

1.21 Washers

21. Bead-making supplies: Sculpey III; Fimo; Cernit; cornstarch; baking soda; fine florist wire (available at craft shops); pasta-making machine; rolling pin; tiny, round cookie cutter

22. Handmade papers or watercolor paper

23. Fabric paints; Rit dye

24. Piece of press-on backing for mounting needlework, heavy cardboard (use either for pin backings)

25. Fine crochet hook for pulling thread or fabric through beads

26. Earring posts, french ear hooks, kidney wires, earring clips, barrette clips, pin backs, eye pins, head pins, jump rings, lobster claw and spring clasps, cones, bead tips,

1.22 Earring posts   *1.23 French ear hook*   *1.24 Kidney wire*

1.25 Earring clip   *1.26 Barrette clips*   *1.27 Pin backs*

1.30 Jump ring

1.28 Eye pin   *1.29 Head pin*   *1.31 Lobster claw clasp set*

1.32 Spring clasp set   *1.33 Cones*

1.34 *Bead tips*

1.35 *Crimp beads*

1.36 *Button covers*

1.37 *Hook and figure-8 eye*

1.38 *Shoe clip*

1.39 *Stick pin set*

crimp beads, button covers, hook and figure-8 eye, shoe clip, stick pin set (all available at craft shops or through mail order)

Now that you're focused on jewelry, you'll analyze everything you see with a jewelry designer's eye: *How can I use it? Where can I use it? Maybe I'll use it next year—I'll take it all.*

It never fails—once you put your mind into a jewelry mode, one idea leads to another, which leads to another, and so on. Your final idea in no way resembles the first, and you may end up with a dozen super inspirations from one mundane thought.

So gather up your supplies and prepare yourself for hours of fun learning to make beads, cords, and clasps. Then put them together into original jewelry you'll love to wear or give away as a special gift. Let's get started!

2. Beads

Beads are integral to jewelry, for the cords you construct, pendants you embroider, and pins you paint. This chapter shows you both how to make beads and how to incorporate home-made and store-bought beads into jewelry.

Visit the library to find clay recipes I didn't include and craft shops to find new clay products that appear regularly.

My favorite store-bought bead sources are thrift shops (you'd be surprised at the treasures you'll find) and the mail-order sources I've listed at the back of this book.

Making clay beads

First we'll make oven-baked clay beads. I've included two different kinds in this chapter: Sculpey III and a clay bead made from cornstarch and baking soda. Sculpey can be painted with acrylics but so many colors are available I've never found that necessary. However, I may wish to draw on a couple dots, stripes, a nose or maybe an eye and I can do this with a permanent marker. I can obtain any color I want by mixing clays of different colors: pastels are created by adding white to colors, or add a bit of black to gray down a color that's too bright. Mix red and orange to get a red/orange or yellow and green to get a sour lime green—the possibilities are endless.

I never throw away Sculpey clay because it doesn't dry out and is reusable. If I have leftover clay from other projects, I use that as a core for the beads I make. The core is covered by thin slices of the designs I make from fresh Sculpey so it is never wasted.

Baking soda beads are colored by kneading Rit dye into them. Try combinations of dye colors or, after working several colors into as many batches of bead dough, combine pieces from each color into one batch to give a marbleized effect.

Using Sculpey III

Sources of Supplies (page 127) lists mail-order companies that supply every type of commercially made bead, but if you want something original, you can make your own.

An excellent medium for bead making is an oven-baked clay called Sculpey III (see Sources of Supplies). I've also used Fimo and Cernit, which resemble Sculpey, and have had wonderful results, but Sculpey III is easier to find in our area, is easily worked, and looks wonderful when finished.

Sculpey III is available in ten basic colors, ten brilliant colors, and ten metallic colors. Purchase single bars, boxes of eight 2-oz. bars, sample boxes of all 30 colors, and multipaks containing ten 2-oz. assorted colors of one set.

Sculpey doesn't air-dry; instead, you make the beads, small sculptures, pins, earrings, and so forth; then place them in a kitchen oven on a low temperature (300 degrees) for approximately ten minutes (the time will depend on the thickness of the item). Only then is the clay dry and hard enough for use. After baking, objects should be painted with liquid acrylic glaze (available where you bought the clay) to intensify color tones and give a glossy or matte finish.

To make Sculpey beads, first cut a clay bar in half, then twist and knead each piece until it's pliable. Combine them, and you're ready to form it into beads, pins, or whatever you wish to sculpt.

If you have a pasta-making machine, prepare the Sculpey by using the following method: First cut the bars into small pieces, then crank them through a pasta machine. After several runs through, combining the slabs, then running it through the machine again, the clay quickly becomes pliable.

The pasta machine is also used for rolling out uniform slabs of clay. You can use a rolling pin, but the thickness of the clay won't be as consistent, and it isn't as easy.

Helen Banes, from Silver Springs, MD, came to the Chicago area and taught a class on Sculpey jewelry. I wanted to make samples of everything we learned, so when my friend, Marilyn, and I spent a week at her home in northern Wisconsin, we took all our Sculpey materials with us and spent our free time making Sculpey jewelry. My black-and-white necklace and Marilyn's Sculpey faces are on the color pages (see Color Plates 1 and 4).

Project 1: Sculpey III necklace

2.1 *Sculpey bead necklace*

Supplies needed:

Clay: 1 box white Sculpey III, 1 box black Sculpey III scraps of Sculpey III (if you have them)

Cord and thread: 1 yd. (.9m) black waxed linen thread

Glue: 527 jeweler's cement or Super Glue

Tools: pasta machine or rolling pin; wallpaper razor blade; florist's wire or fine, double-pointed knitting needle; wire cutter; small, round cookie cutter

Miscellaneous: 24" (61cm) of 3/8" (9.5mm) black rubber hose, one package each of three sizes of colored glass-head pins, large baking pan, waxed paper to work on, alcohol for cleaning tools

Following are simple ways to make beads out of the plain and ordinary. I used them all on my black-and-white necklace.

1. Marble colors by forming cigarlike rolls of two or more colors, placing them side by side,

2.2 *Roll out canes of clay.*

then twisting them together until streaked or marbled. Don't work it too much or the colors combine into one shade.

2.3 *Twist two or more colors and combine to marble.*

2. Roll out long, narrow tubes of colors. Wrap each with a thin layer of another color and place

2.4 *Wrap cane of one color with covering of another.*

seven or eight together; place wedges of color between canes; then wrap

2.5 *Cut one or more canes into wedges.*

the whole bundle with a thin layer of Sculpey. Roll over a flat surface to hold them together and form a flowerlike mille-fiore tube.

2.6 *Place wedges between canes and wrap with clay to make millefiore tube.*

3. Begin making checkerboards by rolling out by hand or by pasta machine, white, then black bars of Sculpey until they are extremely thin (setting number 2 on the pasta machine). Layer these by starting with a white slab, ending with black. Slice the stack into

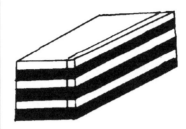

2.7 *Stack black and white slabs of clay and cut into slices.*

1/16" (2mm) thick pieces. Restack those pieces by starting with white, flipping so the next slice is black first. Alternate white and black to make a checker-board.

2.8 *Flip every other slice, then combine into checkerboard.*

4. For another bead, layer black and white slabs as in step 3 and cut down through them to make stripes.

2.9 *Stack different colored slabs and slice for stripes.*

5. Roll out thin canes of white and canes of black, slice them to make polka dots and apply them to the surface of the beads (after covering the bead with a thin layer of black for white polka dots, or white for black polka dots).

2.10 *Slice off thin circles of cane to make polka dots.*

6. Put one piece of marbleized clay (see Fig. 2.3) through the pasta maker again to blend the colors even more; then roll it into a little-finger diameter for a grayer, marbled effect. Make polka dots from this, too.

7. Using the pasta machine, roll out another layer of black and one of white. Stack these on your work table (I work on waxed paper), push down and roll it out (with a rolling pin) until the clay layers stick together. Starting from a long side, roll up a cane from the two colors to look like a pinwheel.

2.11 Stack two different colored clay slabs, roll, and slice into pinwheels.

After preparing the coverings, begin making beads (the bead cores) from Sculpey. Of course you can use black or white for the black-and-white beads, but I use

scrap clay left over from other projects. Always save leftovers. Perhaps the clay has picked up scraps of colors you don't want in it, it's dirty from overworking it, the color is terrible, or it's a failed experiment. These disasters provide the inside, never-seen part of the beads. One word of caution: Don't use red clay for centers as it has a tendency to bleed out into the white—even after baking.

To make the beads, work and roll the scrap clay into a long, chunky roll, then cut it up into the same size pieces for the beads. Roll each bead to make a ball, then line the balls up next to each other to see that the size is correct. Remember, you'll add more clay to the surface when you cover them with slices of designs, so make your beads much smaller than you want the finished bead to be.

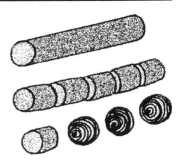

2.12 Roll out large chunk of clay and cut into same sized pieces to roll into beads.

I chose to make all the beads the same size. From the sizes and numbers of beads on previous necklaces, I chose to make an odd number (13) of beads so the necklace has a center front bead and a spacer at the back, and slips over the head.

Each of the beads on my necklace is different. To do this, I used the wallpaper razor to slice thin pieces of marble (1/16" [2mm]), pinwheels, checkerboards, and stripes and applied these to the bead cores. Some were applied all over, others in spots, and some I combined with others. The slices were thin and consistent. Don't be discouraged if a pinwheel goes awry or a checkerboard is not exact. I like that and I think you will, too. When you finish covering a bead, roll it on a hard surface to make it smooth.

Use a tiny, round cookie cutter to cut spacers (I used 26 spacers) from a slab of marbleized clay (1/8" [3mm] thick). Spacers are smaller beads that go between the larger, main, or more important beads to help the necklace hang better and sometimes help set off the other beads. They also add to the overall effect or beauty of the piece.

Push a double-pointed knitting needle or a piece of florist's wire through the center of the beads and spacers to make the holes. Place the wire across a baking pan and put it in the oven to dry (300 degrees for 15 minutes). If you use long wires, you can bake the entire necklace at once and still have room for more.

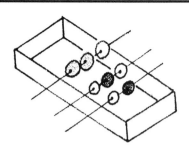

2.13 *Poke florist's wire through beads and place them over a pan to bake in the oven.*

Once the beads are baked dry, let them cool and then coat them with either a matte glaze or shiny glaze (available where you bought the clay). This isn't necessary, but it protects the beads and brings out their design.

In class, Helen showed us a necklace that used pieces of rubber hose with colorful, glass-head pins stuck in it. We had decided to work with black and white Sculpey beads only, but wanted to incorporate a touch of color by stringing on hose beads, too (see Color Plate 4).

Using our handy wallpaper razor, we cut

the hose we purchased at a hardware store into 13 beads, each 3/4" (19mm) long, for each necklace.

Many of the glass-head pins we bought were too long, so Marilyn cut them down with a wire cutter before we pressed them into the hose beads. We left the pins long enough to cross the center and into the hose on the other side, but too short to come out the other side.

To arrange the beads in the necklace, I placed them on a table in front of me and placed a glass-beaded black hose bead between each round Sculpey bead. In between the hose and Sculpey, I placed a spacer. Then I slipped a black 3mm bead between each Sculpey bead and disk spacer.

I used black, waxed linen threaded through a long hand-sewing needle to string my beads. Working the needle through the maze of pins inside the hose looks formidable, but it isn't.

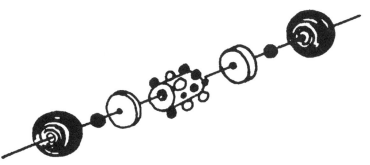

2.14 *Arrange Sculpey beads for a necklace separated by black bead, spacer, glass-beaded black hose bead, spacer, black bead.*

However, we did pay attention to keeping the needle in the middle of the bead as much as possible so the hose would be aligned with the other beads and spacers.

To complete the necklace, I tied a square knot, dotted the knot with glue, and ran the waxed linen back through several beads on both sides before I clipped it off.

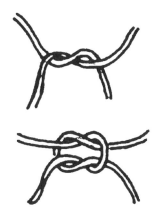

2.15 *Tie a square knot to hold the necklace together.*

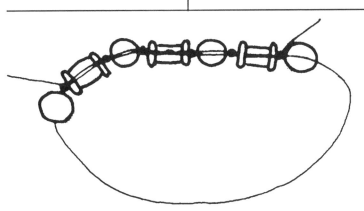

2.16 *Thread cord back through several beads at each side and clip off cord.*

Afterthought: If you need heads, feet, and hands for dolls, buttons or bangles and ornaments for soft jewelry, make them with Sculpey III.

Instant Ideas

1. *Wrap large-hole beads with strings of tiny beads. As you wrap, push beads out of the inside of the hole. Paint glue inside the hole to hold the strings in place.*

2. *When tying knots in a cord on each side of a bead to hold that bead in place on a necklace, use smaller beads on each side of the larger one if it has a hole too big for the knotted cord.*

Making cornstarch beads

When I want beads with a primitive, pottery look, I make cornstarch beads (see Color Plate 5). This is the recipe:

1 cup cornstarch

2 cups baking soda

1-1/4 cups cold water

Place all this in a saucepan, stir together to blend, and cook over medium heat. Keep stirring until the mixture resembles mashed potatoes. Take it off the heat and cover it with a damp cloth until it is cool enough to work with your hands. When cool, divide the recipe into several batches, put on rubber gloves, and add a different color of dry Rit dye to each piece of dough. I used tan, rust, and moss green, controlling the color by the amount of dye I added to each. Beads will be lighter when they are dry.

Knead the dye into each piece of dough, then pull off small pieces of dough to form beads.

2.17 Incise cornstarch beads with a toothpick to decorate them.

Use a toothpick to score some of them, or poke tiny holes into them. Roll them into sand, too, if you wish, for a different finish. Some sand falls away from the beads, but they still retain a primitive, interesting look.

Air-dry these beads slowly (24 to 48 hours). You can place them in the oven on the lowest setting or let the pilot light dry them (the beads will dry in one to two hours).

Instant Ideas

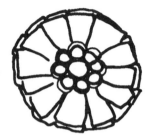

3. *Surround a large button or pin with denim fringe and add a barrette, bolo, or pin backing.*

4. *Make beaded, removable epaulets for a blouse or jacket and attach with Velcro.*

Making vegetable beads

Odd as it sounds, carrots and potatoes make interesting beads (see Indian medicine necklace in Chapter 6). Air-dry or dry them in the oven. I've tried the microwave and was not as successful. In the microwave the carrots became brittle and I couldn't poke a hole through them (but they retained their color and were good eating!). Trying to regulate the microwave was more trouble than placing the vegetables in the oven, turning the oven dial to warm, and forgetting about them until the next day.

To prepare the carrots, first cut off the tops and an inch (1cm) or so off the tip, then brush and clean them. Slice each carrot into pieces. Place all the pieces on a cookie sheet and put that in the oven on the lowest heat setting. Leave them for the day or overnight. The length of time each piece takes to dry will vary with the size of the carrot piece.

2.18 Cut top and bottom off carrot, then slice carrots for beads.

As the carrot pieces dry, the centers separate from the outsides and can be pushed out. That leaves a large hole for stringing.

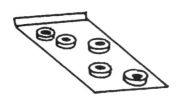

2.19 Place carrots on a cookie sheet and dry in the oven.

The carrots turn wrinkled and brown and you can paint them, if you wish, but I like them left a natural color. I don't

2.20 Carrots shrivel and brown when dried.

spray them with clear acrylic either, but a protective coating may keep them from absorbing humidity. I live in an area of high humidity in the summer, but my beads look just as good in the summer as winter, even though they may feel slightly rubbery.

Potato beads are treated differently. After peeling the potatoes, cut them into different sizes and shapes, poke or cut a hole in the centers and dry them as you do the carrots.

2.21 Peel potato, slice, then cut out potato beads.

All the vegetable pieces shrink considerably when dried, so you may want to experiment with sizes and shapes.

Making fabric beads

Wrapping and winding fabric beads

I've placed fabric beads in three categories: wrapped, wound, and sewn. To wrap beads, use narrow strips of fabric and wrap around a wooden bead or cotton ball until the bead looks like a small ball of fabric.

Or wind strips (the shape and size of the strip determines the shape and size of the beads) around a toothpick or drinking straw. Craft Beader, a relatively new gizmo, is available by mail order. To use one of those, wrap fabric or paper on the long cotter pins supplied. Different diameters are included so the hole in the bead can be regulated, too.

When making fabric beads, use lightweight fabrics that drape well because both ends of the beads must be gathered easily. But the beads can be decorated any number of ways. I used decorative machine stitches, but you may want to decorate with beads, buttons, sequins, or ribbons.

Afterthought:

Have fun with the children, or use the following as entertainment for a little girl's birthday party. Thread up darning needles with dental floss and let the girls string candy. Choose Life Savers and snaps with holes for easy stringing, and soft types like salt water taffy, licorice, jelly beans, and gum drops.

Another jewelry idea for children is stringing pasta on dental floss or stiff cord. Buy different shapes and sizes. Leave it plain or dye it with a food color (one part) and isopropyl (rubbing) alcohol (two parts) mixture. I use a covered glass jar, drop the pasta into a color, shake it up and use a slotted spoon to take it out and spread on several layers of paper towel to dry. Wash out the jar and mix up another color.

Instant Ideas

5. *Make removable appliqués. Cover with beads, then stretch over batting-covered cardboard shapes and glue down edges. Sew a pin to the back of a piece of Ultrasuede, glue to the cardboard, then cut back edges with a pinking shears so they extend slightly beyond the appliqué.*

6. *Bead, wrap, and embroider your own hero medals. Don't stop at one, but make a whole fruit salad for your outfit.*

Project 2:
Wrapped and wound denim necklace

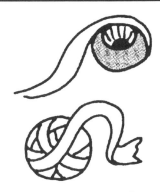

2.23 *Wrap fabric around wooden beads.*

2.22 *String beads and spacers in this order: large denim beads in the center front, each separated by six flannel disks. Repeat with smaller beads and spacers on each side.*

The denim necklace (see Color Plate 16) uses both wrapped and wound beads. To make them, I gathered up the following supplies:

Fabric: scraps of blue denim, 1/2 yd. (46cm) red flannel

Bead centers: three cotton balls or three large-hole macramé beads

Cord and thread: waxed linen or dental floss

Tools: doll needle, embroidery scissors, fine crochet hook, rotary cutting wheel and mat, toothpick or Craft Beader

Miscellaneous: lingerie drying bag, tacky glue, white glue and brush, clasp and two jump rings

Cut the fabric into 1/4"-3/8" (.6-1cm) strips. Wrap fabric strips around wooden beads. Of course, that method does present a problem later—that of finding the hole for stringing. Use a macramé bead for this and you can feel the hole later (it is always large). The problem with macramé beads is that they are also usually large.

An alternative way to wrap, if the bead holes are large enough (macramé beads), is wrapping the fabric through the centers and around the outside to cover the beads. Or use

2.24 *Wrap fabric through center of beads.*

cotton balls as centers and wrap fabric around them. They lend no weight, and usually the beads are easy to string if you use a sharp needle.

For the denim necklace I wrapped five beads over macramé beads, with the rest (20 beads) wound on a Craft Beader (see Fig. 1.14), or you can substitute a toothpick. Start

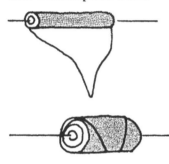

2.25 Wind fabric around toothpicks to make beads.

with a triangle 8" (20cm) long and 1-1/2" (4cm) wide. The end of the strip is dotted with tacky glue to hold it in place.

Audrey Griese of Champlin, MN, has been making denim beads for years. She suggested I mix up a jar of white craft

2.26 Clip around edges of red flannel disks.

glue and water (one part glue to three parts water) and paint the denim beads after wrapping. I liked this idea because the coating is not so thick that it is noticeable on the beads, yet it helps hold the beads together as well as protect them from dirt. I painted the beads with glue, and while I waited for them to dry (low heat in the oven helps speed the process), I made the red flannel spacers.

For spacers, I cut out red flannel disks, using a penny as a pattern. Then I soaked them in water, placed them in a bag used

for drying lingerie, and tossed them in a dryer to dry the flannel and soften the edges.

Place the dry beads in front of you on a table in stringing order. Assemble the necklace, using a doll needle and dental floss or waxed linen. String one denim and six flannel disks, then repeat these steps until all the beads and spacers are in place (end with beads). Attach a closure to the ends (see Chapter 4), or make the necklace long enough to slip over your head.

Finally, make small clips around the flannel edges to fringe the red disks.

Project 3: Denim earrings

Use wound beads to make matching earrings (see Color Plate 16). You need:

Fabric: denim scraps
Thread: blue sewing thread
Tools: needle-nosed pliers, Craft Beader or toothpick, hand-sewing needle
Miscellaneous: 1 yd. (.9m) tiny red rick-rack, white craft glue, two jump rings, two eye pins, two french hook earring findings

First wrap tiny red rick-rack around a 1"-wide (2.5cm-wide) piece of cardboard, six times. Use blue polyester thread and a hand needle to tie the hank together at the top and attach it to an eye pin.

2.27 Tie a hank of rick-rack at the top .

2.28 Attach top to an eye pin.

Wind up two denim beads over a toothpick from a triangle of denim 8" (20cm) long and 1-1/2" (4cm) wide. Insert an eye pin at one end of the bead

2.29 Insert eye pin into bead.

and pull the hank of rick-rack up inside about 1/4" (6mm). Slip the eye pin through an earring finding and, using needle-nosed pliers, bend the eye pin down, back inside the bead.

2.30 Finish earring by bending the eye pin over the earring finding.

Project 4:
Brocade ribbon necklace

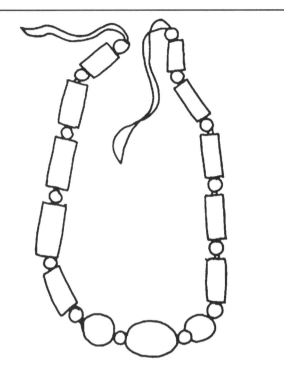

2.31 Assemble the beads in this order, using small brass beads as spacers, three larger, ornate brass beads in the center.

These beads are made by winding brocade ribbon around plastic drinking straws. (Instead of ribbon, try wallpaper [see Color Plates 8 and 13], wrapping paper, or slick magazine pages.)

Ribbon: 18" (47cm) each of five ribbons, 1 yd. (.9m) of 3/8"-wide (9.5mm-wide) teal blue double-faced satin ribbon

Beads: 14 brass beads for spacers, 3 large brass beads for center front, 20 brass washers (5/8" [16mm] diameter)

Glue: Goop

Tools: fabric shears, fine crochet hook

Miscellaneous: Fray Check, several large plastic straws

I had five pieces of brocade ribbon from another project I'd finished a year ago. None of the pieces was longer than 18" (46cm). I cut each piece of ribbon in half. After wrapping the first bead, I discovered the ribbon wasn't long enough to make the bead as plump as I wanted it. My solution was to glue the end of each piece to a large plastic drinking straw (this increased the size of the bead and I could easily string the ribbon through the center).

Before I began gluing and wrapping, I cut the straws the same size as the ribbon widths (these varied from 1" [2.5cm] to 1-1/2" [4cm]). Then I glued a piece of ribbon to a straw, wound up the ribbon, and glued down the end with Goop. (I

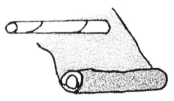

2.32 Glue ribbon to a piece of plastic drinking straw.

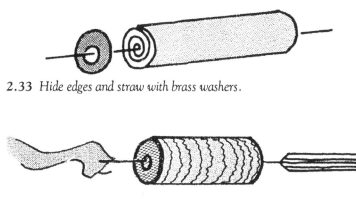

2.33 Hide edges and straw with brass washers.

2.34 Use a crochet hook to pull the ribbon through the beads.

chose Goop because it doesn't soak through and stain the ribbon.) I followed the same procedure with each piece of ribbon.

At the edge of each bead, I hid the ribbon and straw edges by gluing brass washers to them. I combined my brocade beads with brass beads (these were purchased as part of a necklace at an import shop).

First I placed the beads in front of me and arranged them as I wanted to string them on the satin ribbon. Then I used a fine crochet hook to pull the ribbon through each bead and tied the ends at back in a bow. To keep the ribbon from raveling, I spread a dot of Fray Check at the cut edges.

7. *Make removable beaded collars and cuffs for blouses and jackets or crew neck, long-sleeved sweaters.*

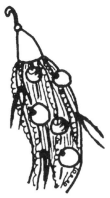

8. *Make a necklace with strips of Ultrasuede, threads, cords, yarn, and strings of beads. Sew paillettes to the yarn, and add more beads and bangles.*

Sewing fabric beads

Project 5:
Pillow bead necklace

2.35 Pillow Bead Necklace

The decorative stitches on my new sewing machine intrigued me. I decided to make sample strips of some of them using silky fabrics combined with rayons and metallics for thread, then combining them with brass beads to make a silky, embroidered pillow bead necklace (see Color Plates 13 and 14).

First I gathered together silky fabrics in fuchsia, purple, red, and teal fabrics. Then I chose some threads that clashed with the fabric colors, some that matched the fabrics, and others that were obvious go-togethers.

I purchased a brass bead necklace at an import shop sale and took it apart for the spacer beads and closure (I used other parts of it for the brocade necklace).

Supplies needed:
Beads: 8 brass rondelles (diameter about 16mm), 2 brass tubes (about 1 1/2" x 1/2" [4cm x 1.5cm]), 2 round brass beads, 1 brass closure
Strips of fabric:
    fuchsia: one strip 4" x 6" (10cm x 15cm) (for 1 bead)

purple: one strip 4" x 10" (10cm x 25.5cm) (for 2 beads)
red: one strip 4" x 10" (10cm x 25.5cm) (for 2 beads)
teal: one strip 4" x 8" (10cm x 20.5cm) (for 2 beads)
Threads: rayon machine embroidery in kelly green, red, yellow, purple, fuchsia, teal, orange, gold metallic, beading thread
Miscellaneous: vanishing marker, fiberfill, freezer paper or adding machine tape, doll needle, waxed linen, beading cord

If you use freezer paper as a stabilizer, press strips of it to the backs of all the fabric strips. Lightly fold the strips in half. If

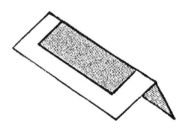

2.36 Fold fabric and ironed-on freezer paper down the center.

Plate 1

Clockwise from top left. ■ Machine-embroidered pin. ■ Satin-stitch necklace, hung with Guatemalan worry dolls. ■ Collar tube necklace with Sculpey pin. ■ Worry doll earrings (*also shown at lower left*) match satin-stitch necklace. ■ Instant button earrings. ■ Use leftover fabric from pillow beads to make a barrette. ■ Artist **Jane Warnick** of Houston machine embroidered on water-soluble stabilizer to make this necklace.

Plate 2

Clockwise from top left. ■ Fluffy boa, made of fabric strips, rick-rack, ribbon, yarn and cord. ■ Old buttons decorate a wide bracelet. ■ Artist **dj Bennett** of Lake Forest, Ill., machine stitched cuffs of glitzy fabrics covered with black tulle. ■ Use beads to quilt flowers on a barrette. ■ Old buttons create new pins. ■ Buttons, beads, and feathers decorate funky doll pins.

Plate 3

Clockwise from top left. ■ Ready-made hoop earrings wrapped with strips of leftover silk. ■ Artist **Judi Maddigan** of San Jose, Calif., uses a serger to incorporate beads into a narrow rolled hem cord *(also shown at far left).* ■ Cutout pictures are glued to backings and finished with casting resin. ■ Recycled embroidery, cut, shaped, beaded and stuffed. ■ Alternating silk bead tube. ■ Glitzy doll pin. ■ Braided tube. ■ Woven strips of handmade paper make colorful earrings.

Plate 4

Clockwise from top left. ■ Knot furry yarn for minestrone necklace. ■ Button earrings with soutache, beads, sequins. ■ Sculpey tube bead strung with velour idiot cord. ■ Earrings and necklace made of Sculpey ovenbaked clay. ■ Fabric tube made of man's tie, strung with beads. ■ Beaded barrette.

you use adding machine tape for a stabilizer, first finger press the strips of fabric in half the long way and then open them again and back each with adding machine tape before you proceed to stitch.

With a vanishing marker, draw a line down the fold. This is the first stitching line and the center of the beads. Then draw lines indicating the width of each strip. The

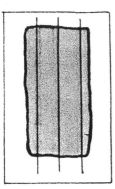

2.37 *Draw lines down the center fold and at each side of the bead.*

beads are not only different widths, but different lengths as well. Stitch on strips much longer than needed so you can match motifs, if you wish, when stitching the strips into tubes.

The finished *cut* sizes are:

1 fuchsia bead—
2-1/4" x 3- 1/2"
(6cm x 9cm);
2 purple beads, each
2-1/4" x 4"
(6cm x 10cm);
2 red beads, each
2-1/2" x 3-1/2"
(6.5cm x 9cm);
2 teal beads, each
2-1/2" x 2-3/4"
(6.5cm x 7cm).

Embroider within these areas:

fuchsia, 1-1/4" x 3"
(3cm x 8cm);
purple, 1-1/4" x 3-1/2"
(3cm x 9cm);
red, 1-1/2" x 3"
(4cm x 8cm);
teal, 1-1/2 x 2-1/4"
(4cm x 6cm).

Choose decorative stitches and combinations of stitches found on your sewing machine. It's best to use contrasting or clashing colors down the

center lines. Choose a symmetrical stitch such as a star burst or feather stitch for the centers.

Change to another color and another decorative stitch and stitch down at either side of the center. Use the presser foot as a guide to keep the stitching lines straight.

Leave that thread on the machine and choose another strip of fabric to use this same color down the center line. Then change thread and sew down the center of the next bead. Can this thread be used on either of the other two strips you've sewn? If so, don't waste time threading and rethreading—use the same color. Go on to the next strip and another color, and then use that color, if possible, on another bead. Continue in this manner until you've filled the area needed for each bead (see measurements above).

Once that is completed, go back and stitch triple straight stitches of gold metallic thread between stitches already in place. At the sides of the beads along the drawn lines I like using a "buttonhole" stitch and the mirror of it at the other side. Go beyond the edges with an open-type stitch and fill in the area that will be gathered. Steer clear of heavy

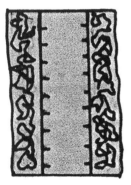

2.38 *Use a stitch like the buttonhole within 1/2" (13mm) of each side. Then fill in beyond the buttonhole stitches with embroidery.*

satin stitches so the gathers will look smooth, not bulky.

When finished, remove as much of the stabilizer as you can from the sides of the strips. Then cut the strips in two if they are two beads long. Check on the dimensions and cut off any excess fabric.

With right sides together, use your machine to sew tubes from these strips (1/4" [6mm] seam allowance). Fold in

2.39 *Sew strips into tubes.*

at least 1/8" (3mm) at the remaining raw edges and sew a running stitch (gathering stitch) by hand around each opening right at the fold. Pull

2.40 *Fold in ends and sew a running stitch in the fold.*

up and stitch again invisibly around one of the openings and anchor by stitching in one place to keep the tube closed.

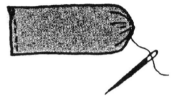

2.41 *Pull up and finish one side. Fill with batting.*

Using fiberfill or batting, fill the tube tightly. Then pull up on the gathering stitches on the other end, stitch around again, poking in the raw edges. You've made one bead. Proceed with all the others in the same way.

2.42 *Gather up other side to complete bead.*

Once you've finished this, assemble your necklace as shown in Fig. 2.35.

Now that you know how to make pillow beads, make other necklaces by varying the dimensions, colors, fabric, or adding beads or sequins to the beads. You can add a long pillow bead to each side instead of using small ones.

2.43 *Use longer beads at the sides for another look.*

Using glass beads

It isn't always necessary or advantageous to make your own beads. Sometimes only glass, metal, bone, shell, or plastic will do. The variety available today is extraordinary, as you will see if you thumb through bead catalogs (see Sources of Supplies).

Commercial beads come in all sizes, shapes, and colors. On the first beading project I've stitched by hand bugle beads, smooth seed beads, and small faceted beads to imitate an antique beaded appliqué I own.

The second beading project is also stitched by hand. Quilting with beads isn't a new idea, but the flowered barrette is a small accessory that looks like quilting—or smocking—gone wild. It's a technique you can use for other jewelry, too.

Instant Idea

9. *Buy plastic headbands and decorate them by wrapping them with fabric. On some, glue on worry dolls, buttons, beads, bows, and charms.*

Attaching beads by hand

Project 6: Beaded necklace from appliqué pattern

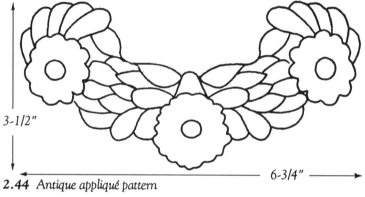

3-1/2"

6-3/4"

2.44 *Antique appliqué pattern*

I was taking a beading class when I found a beaded, embroidered appliqué at an antique store. I decided to copy this design and use my new knowledge to bead the design. I put the appliqué on a copy machine and made the pattern (see Color Plate 8).

Using transfer paper between the copy and a scrap of black Ultrasuede, I used an empty ball-point pen to transfer the image to the Ultrasuede, then outlined the design with a running stitch of white thread.

Seed beads often have tiny holes that won't accommodate regular hand-sewing needles, so you must use beading needles. They come in many sizes. When you choose beading needles, threads and beads, you must match needle to bead, and thread to needle. The lower the needle number, the thicker the needle. For example, a number 10 beading needle is thicker than a number 16. Bead-ing thread comes in sizes too (size "A" is finer than size "F," which is heavy and used for number 10 beading needles).

Beading needles have eyes that sometimes seem impossible to thread. You may be able to use a needle threader, should you have trouble threading the fine needle eyes, but I have a helpful hint for you. First, clip the thread off clean. You know how you are tempted to put the end of the thread in your mouth to wet it? Well, put the eye of the needle in your mouth instead and wet the end of it. Place the thread up to the eye and it is drawn through the needle as if by magic.

Use a fine beading needle and doubled black polyester thread or black beading thread for this appliqué. To bead the appliqué, I used a method where three beads are

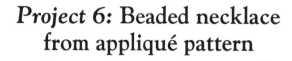

2.45 *Slip needle through three beads, stitch into fabric, back and up again to slip the needle through the last two beads. Then slip on three more beads and proceed as before.*

strung on the needle, the needle is poked down through the fabric and is brought back under the fabric, then up through the fabric and the last two beads again. Load your needle with three more beads and repeat the process. This keeps the beads hugging the fabric. You can also apply two beads at a time using the same method. You

2.46 Slip needle through two beads, stitch into fabric, back and up again to slip the needle through the last one bead.

can also stitch down one at a time and sometimes you have to (see flower

2.47 Stitch down one bead at a time without an anchoring stitch.

barrette below). Or work with two threads, holding the beads on one thread while couching down between the beads with another thread.

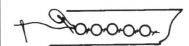

2.48 String beads on one thread, then stitch thread in place between beads with another needle and thread (couching).

Supplies needed:

Fabric: Ultrasuede 9" x 6" (23cm x 15cm)

Beads: I bought a hank of each color, though I didn't need all of them: copper bugle beads, small faceted dark brown beads, iridescent brown/blue seed beads, transparent teal, clear glass, rust, and light brown seed beads

Thread: black polyester sewing thread, white sewing thread

Needle: beading needles to fit beads

Cord: 24" (61cm) silky, heavy monk's cord

Glue: Goop

Miscellaneous: empty ballpoint pen, transfer paper, beauty pin (small bar pin used in heirloom sewing instead of button) (optional)

The beads I chose are not all the same size— strings of beads are sometimes like that. But the inconsistency itself is

consistent and interesting. In this necklace, flower centers are transparent teal seed beads, leaves are copper bugle beads, and for outlining areas I used iridescent brown/blue seed beads. Three bead colors are mixed for the flowers (clear, transparent rust, and light brown beads). The mixture included twice as many clear beads as the other two and I chose them at random as I beaded.

Each string of beads was spilled into a separate jar lid. This makes putting beads on the needle much easier and jar lids don't tip over.

I began beading by outlining the flower centers; next, I outlined the flowers; then I outlined the leaves with the iridescent brown/blue beads. Once outlined, I went back and filled in the areas as shown. The most important rule is: don't crowd the rows of beads (or you'll find them popping up above the surface as you apply row after row).

When beading is completed, slip the cord

2.49 *Lines in the pattern indicate the direction of the threads as you bead.*

around your neck and make it long enough so you don't need a closure. If you need the pendant shorter for some garments, use a tiny beauty pin to pin the cord together at the correct length in back.

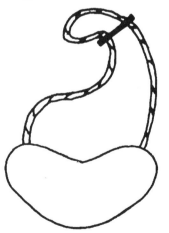

2.50 *Shorten the necklace with a beauty pin.*

To finish, cut out the beaded shape from the Ultrasuede. Glue the cord ends with Goop adhesive and flatten the ends to the Ultrasuede.

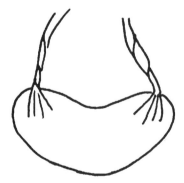

2.51 *Flatten cord ends when you glue the cord in place.*

Then cover the entire back of the appliqué with Goop and apply it to another piece of black Ultrasuede. Cut back the Ultrasuede backing to match the appliqué. Use

clip clothespins to hold the pieces together until the next day, when the adhesive is dry.

Finish the necklace by beading the edge with iridescent brown/blue beads. To do this, use a doubled thread and beading needle. Knot the end and hide the knot near the edge. Slip on two beads, then stitch down into the suede from front to back (slant the needle back between the beads when you poke your needle through the two pieces of suede), come back through the second bead again, and add two more beads. Continue till the edge is finished.

2.52 *When beading the edge, slip needle through two beads, slant needle back from front to back through both suede layers, then slip the needle through the last bead. Add two more beads and proceed.*

More decorative edges are found in beading books, but this method suited the appliqué, and I wanted the beads to be tight to the edge.

Project 7: Quilted and beaded flower barrette

The flowers on this barrette (see Color Plate 2) are based on an idea from a 1920s book of hat and garment decoration, and they're still fresh-looking today. I used beads to quilt it.

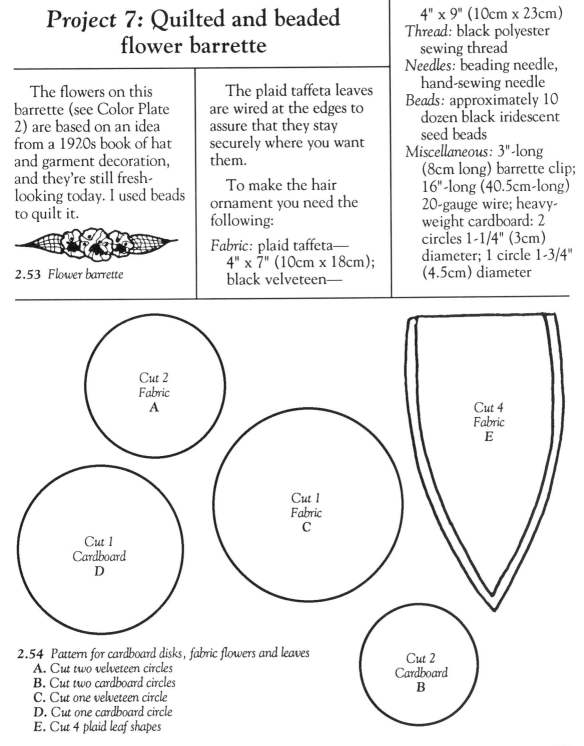

2.53 *Flower barrette*

The plaid taffeta leaves are wired at the edges to assure that they stay securely where you want them.

To make the hair ornament you need the following:

Fabric: plaid taffeta—4" x 7" (10cm x 18cm); black velveteen—4" x 9" (10cm x 23cm)
Thread: black polyester sewing thread
Needles: beading needle, hand-sewing needle
Beads: approximately 10 dozen black iridescent seed beads
Miscellaneous: 3"-long (8cm long) barrette clip; 16"-long (40.5cm-long) 20-gauge wire; heavyweight cardboard: 2 circles 1-1/4" (3cm) diameter; 1 circle 1-3/4" (4.5cm) diameter

Cut 2
Fabric
A

Cut 4
Fabric
E

Cut 1
Fabric
C

Cut 1
Cardboard
D

Cut 2
Cardboard
B

2.54 *Pattern for cardboard disks, fabric flowers and leaves*
  A. *Cut two velveteen circles*
  B. *Cut two cardboard circles*
  C. *Cut one velveteen circle*
  D. *Cut one cardboard circle*
  E. *Cut 4 plaid leaf shapes*

Cut out three velveteen flowers, one large and two smaller, and four plaid leaves following the patterns provided; also cut out the three cardboard circles.

Sew a running stitch 1/4" (6mm) inside the edge of one of the velveteen circles. Place the

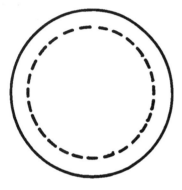

2.55 Sew a running stitch inside edge of circle.

cardboard circle (note sizes) inside the fabric and draw up at the edge. The velvet will balloon slightly on the topside. It may help if you dot the

back edge with glue stick. As you draw up the thread, push the folds into place evenly around the edge. Stitch in place several times to anchor

2.56 Draw up the fabric edge over the cardboard shape.

the thread. Follow the same directions for the other two velveteen flowers.

Thread up again with a regular sewing needle and stitch the fabric on the topside to the cardboard in several spots. This gives the velvet a lovely

2.57 Stitch down velveteen to cardboard.

texture. The stitches go through the cardboard from back to front and back again. This is easily done without breaking needles if you use a thimble and push the needle through evenly and slowly. If you have a hard, mar-proof surface to work on, then hold the needle, needle-eye down on the work surface, point up with fabric-covered cardboard on top, and push down to work the needle through.

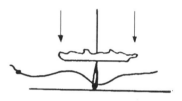

2.58 Push covered cardboard down on a needle.

Complete the three flowers. Then use a beading needle to stitch down seed beads one at a time on top of the quilting. In the centers, string about a dozen beads on the thread and stitch

2.59 *Cover stitches with beads, then string and stitch down three bead loops for flower centers.*

back down in the same place to create a loop of beads. Stitch three loops in the center of each flower.

To make the leaves, stitch right sides together. Then go back and zigzag stitch (stitch width 3, stitch length 1.5) in the seam allowance over the wire to hold it in

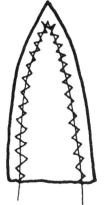

2.60 *Straight stitch right sides together first, then zigzag stitch over wire along the straight stitching.*

place (use an embroidery foot or a presser foot grooved deeply enough to let the wire feed through smoothly). To turn it to the right side, start from the point and roll the leaf down to the other end. Turn it right side out as you unroll the leaf. This is not as hard as it sounds.

2.61 *Roll up the leaf, then turn it right side out.*

Thread up the sewing needle again with a thread at least 36" (.9m) long. Double it for strength and sew the leaves to the barrette as shown, gathering the base of the leaves slightly.

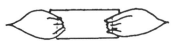

2.62 *Gather leaves at the open ends, then stitch to barrette.*

Then sew the flowers together. The center

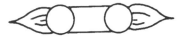

2.63 *Sew two flowers at the sides over the leaves.*

flower will overlap the ones at the sides. Those

2.64 *Place large flower in center and stitch it in place.*

will overlap the leaves. Stitch the flowers in place by using long stitches from one side of the flowers across the inside of the barrette to the other and back again. Stitch down the end holes of the barrette to the leaves. When completed, bend the leaves into the desired shape.

Afterthought: Use these flowers singly—with or without small leaves—for shoe ornaments, or make a button from one. Make small earrings to match. Don't limit yourself to circles only. Make a smocked rectangle for a barrette.

Attaching beads by machine

Couching down beads can be done by machine, too, but massing beads as I did on the beaded necklace precludes the machine—for me. I think it is much easier doing that by hand. However, never rule out anything unless you try it yourself. I like working at the machine when attaching single beads or single strands, but you may want to work at the machine exclusively.

To attach single beads by machine, be sure the hole in the bead is large enough and your needle fine enough. Use either the zigzag or straight stitch method both of which follow:

For either method, first place a dot of glue on the bead to hold it until it's sewn in place. Lower or cover the feed dogs and remove the presser foot.

To zigzag the bead in place, first set the machine on needle left and place needle in the center hole of the bead. Then hand-walk the machine as you regulate the stitch width to find one where the needle clears the width of the bead edge. Remember that setting. You are now ready to sew the bead in place.

Begin by setting the stitch width to 0 and stitching several times in one place to anchor your thread. Next, change to the stitch width you chose previously to clear the bead's rim width. Zigzag stitch several times back and forth over the rim to attach the bead. End in the bead center and change stitch width back to 0 and anchor the thread again. (This is the same as sewing buttons on by machine.)

Or you can attach the bead by straight stitching. To do this, set your machine on stitch width 0 and anchor the thread in the center of the bead by stitching in place three or four times. Raise the needle. Move the fabric over to anchor the thread on the side of the bead. Go back to the center and anchor again. Repeat until the bead is securely sewn in place and will stand up. Nudge the bead to stand on its outside rim when you finish stitching. Wipe off any glue that's noticeable.

2.65 *Stitch bead down by machine at one side and nudge it to stand on edge.*

If you stitch down the other side as well, your bead will lay flat, hole up.

2.66 Stitch down at both sides so hole is up.

Attaching seed beads, or other fine or oddly shaped beads, can be done in the following way: First string the beads onto a thread. Using monofilament in the machine, stitch one end of the beaded thread down on the fabric. Stitch along the thread the width of one bead. Push the first bead near that end and then stitch over the threads to keep the bead in place. Stitch again the distance of the next bead. Push the bead up to the first, stitch over the thread and repeat, as shown in Fig. 2.67.

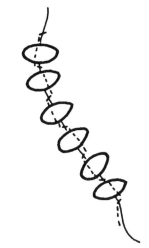

2.67 String beads, then sew between as shown.

Or, sew beads down by stringing them singly on thick threads and stitching both ends of the threads.

You can attach beads invisibly, using mono-filament thread to couch them down or string the beads on. Or choose thread wisely and use the stitches as part of the decoration.

2.68 Place thread through bead and stitch down at each side.

Other products usable for beads or beadmaking include: seeds, shells, rose petals, papier-mâché, bread dough, potter's clay, plaster, crochet thread for bobbles, macramé cord for knots, not to mention all the products you can pur-chase at craft stores or rock shops.

Now that you know how to make and attach beads, turn to Chapter 3 where you'll learn about cords. Then you can attach the beads you've made to your original necklaces, bracelets, stick pins, and other jewelry.

Instant Ideas

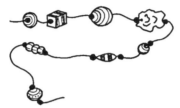

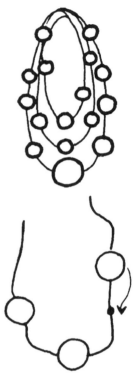

10. Stuff tubes with fiberfill until stiff, or use craft cord inside. Then wrap the stiff, filled tube with strings of beads à la Africa.

12. Make an eclectic necklace with leather cord and all your odd, unmatched beads. Knot at each side of each bead to hold them in place.

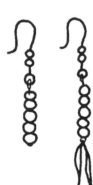

11. Make instant earrings by stringing beads onto head pins, then twisting the top of the pin around an earring hook. Or use eye pins and string decorative cord or thread strung with more beads to the eye.

13. Buy beaded Chinese Christmas ornaments and string them on heavy gold cord.

14. For a summer look, string cork fishing bobbers on leather cord long enough to wrap around your neck two or three times. Knot wherever you want a bobber, then slip the bobber over the knot and drip glue into the hole to hold the bobbers in place on the cord.

3. Cords

Cords are essential to necklaces. Sometimes the cord may be the necklace itself, but often it's a means to the end of displaying buttons, beads, and bangles. You can cover a cord with fabric, thread, or beads, or leave it merely a cord. Other times cords aren't necklaces at all: They're spiraled into earrings, bent into pins, or looped on to shoe clips.

Best of all, you can make the cords for soft jewelry on your serger and sewing machine. Read the following ideas; then spend a day experimenting with cords and threads of different weights, textures, and colors. Record your results in a notebook. Afterwards, go one step further, as I did, and make a sampler necklace. The blue-and-gold necklace (see Color Plate 12) is made from serged and sewn cords. It's a reference for me, and the best part is that I can also wear it.

Covering cords with thread

Using the serger

I'll show you how to create thread-covered cord by using a serger. You can incorporate beads into the cords, too, in a technique you'll find challenging and rewarding.

Project 8: Serged and beaded necklace

When my friend, Judi Maddigan, of San Jose, CA, learned that I was writing a jewelry book, she asked if I'd be interested in her serged-cords-and-beads idea. Was I! We agreed that we hadn't seen this idea before in any other book or periodical.

3.1 A necklace of serged cord with beads

Judi incorporates beads into a cord *as she serges it.*

Directions for two of Judi's necklaces (see Color Plate 3) follow. Both necklaces need 6-lb.-test fishing line. (DMC pearl cotton #5 works, too, but tends to twist.) Both also need beads 2mm or larger (check directions) to string on the fishing line.

Supplies needed for the lavender necklace:

Thread: three spools each Sulky 30 machine embroidery thread #1122, #1080, #1121; one spool of metallic #7012

Miscellaneous: two cones; two jump rings; clasp set; 6-lb.-test fishing line; three dozen 2mm or larger beads

Thread to make the turquoise necklace includes three spools each of Sulky 30, #1045, #1094, #1049, and #1090.

You will string the beads on a filler cord, serge over the cord alone, and periodically move a bead from your lap along the filler cord to the back of the serger foot. Magic! The bead is incorporated into the necklace.

Adjust your serger for a rolled hem with Sulky 30 in the right needle and both loopers. Begin with three different thread colors to simplify tension adjustments. Raise knife if possible. Your serger is ready. Now you must determine the necklace length. To do this, drape a tape measure around your neck to find the length you prefer.

First thread all beads in the order you want on the filler cord (fishing line or DMC pearl cotton). Don't cut the filler cord. The beads will sit in your lap. When you start to serge, serge a thread chain for several inches over only the filler cord so no beads will lay against the back of your neck.

Now follow one of the three methods below. They include directions for using different bead sizes, starting with the largest:

Method A (beads 3mm and over):

1. Raise foot.

2. Pull filler cord to the left under the foot.

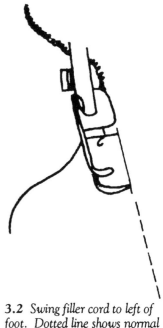

3.2 Swing filler cord to left of foot. Dotted line shows normal position for feeding filler cord.

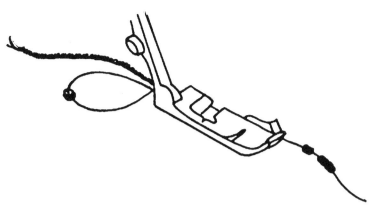

3.3 Slide bead up and behind serger foot forming loop, then serge over filler cord.

3. Lower the foot and take several stitches without catching the filler cord. (Experiment with two to five stitches, depending on the size and shape of the bead.) Raise foot again.

4. Slide one bead up the filler cord and swing it to the left of the foot, forming a loop of filler cord.

5. Lower the foot and continue to serge over the filler cord for about 1" (or until the loop clears the back of the foot).

6. Raise the foot. To eliminate the excess cord in the loop, pull on the free filler cord in front of the foot. The bead will be snug against the serger chain.

Repeat steps two through six until chain reaches the desired length. End with several inches of unbeaded chain. Each necklace is made up of 20 cords, several each of the different colors.

Then join strands and finish ends with jewelry findings. (One option is to knot the cords to eye pins and cement or glue them inside cones.) Twist necklace to wear.

Method B (beads 2 mm to 3mm):

Follow the directions for Method A, omitting steps 2 and 3. If the finished cord kinks too

much, follow the complete set of Method A directions, taking only one stitch without catching the filler cord in step 3.

Method C (beads less than 2mm):

Thread beads on 6-lb.-test fishing line. Feed the filler cord over the front of the foot. To attach a bead, stop with the needle up. Pull on the serged chain slightly as if you were starting to clear the stitch finger. Slide one bead up the filler cord and slip it behind the spot where the needle will form the next stitch. (Use tweezers for tiny beads.) Turn the hand wheel manually until the needle passes the bead and secures it. Continue serging, feeding beads as desired. The beads readily slip under the rear of the foot, eliminating the need to raise it.

Hint: Play with the tensions for different effects. Mix and match thread colors and types. Use metallic threads sparingly because they can feel scratchy against your skin.

Eliminate kinks in the finished, beaded fishing line with a warm hair dryer set on medium temperature. Do not use a hot setting—metallic beads will melt the fishing line.

Camouflage skipped stitches with a dot of Fray Check. Twist the extra loop of thread into an appropriate location and allow to dry.

Loosen the presser foot tension (over three full turns), making it easier to repeatedly raise and lower the foot (optional).

Audrey Griese's serged cords

Audrey Griese also uses the serger for her cord idea. Place heavy thread or cord in the upper looper. Prepare the serger for a narrow rolled hem (use three threads and eliminate the left needle). See your serger manual for instructions for your machine.

By using a heavy cord in the upper looper, you create a rick-rack look. But if you stitch over a filler cord, you create a different, thicker cord. You can either raise the serger blade or leave it down to use as a guide for the filler cord. Hold the filler cord up so it is between the needle and the blade.

Using the sewing machine

With the sewing machine, you can zigzag over pearl cotton for various effects. Use gold thread in the bobbin, and shiny rayon machine embroidery thread on top to decorate the cord.

Use the same technique to satin stitch over embroidery floss to combine sections of it or sew the floss together into a heavy cord. Or, instead of embroidery floss, satin stitch over florist's wire and bend it into a free-form shape for a pin.

Instant Ideas

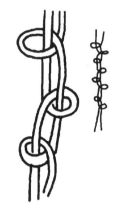

1. *Knot alternate half-hitches in cords and attach ornaments to the loops. Use thick cord to half hitch a belt.*

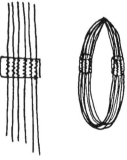

2. *Hold cord or suede strips in place by zigzagging them down side by side on suede squares or rectangles. Glue the fabric into a tube and wear as a necklace— also, fill tube with other suede or cord strips.*

Plate 5
Clockwise from 10 o'clock. ■ Pheasant feather lapel pin. ■ Cut hooks off fishing flies for instant earrings (*see also 2 o'clock*). ■ Brass disk pendant. ■ Embroidered print fabric pendant. ■ Pheasant feathers glued to Ultrasuede, then decorated with beads to make hat ornament. ■ Cornstarch beads look like pottery.

Plate 6
Left and center: Artist **Sherry Boemmel** of Prospect Heights, Ill., made the three macramé desert pins. ■ *Top right:* Artist **dj Bennett** covered scraps of glitzy fabric with clear plastic and stitched by machine. ■ *Lower right:* Artist **Judy Mayo** of Naperville, Ill., used pearl cotton and beads to create off-loom woven neckpiece. ■ *Lower left:* Colorful beads chosen at random fill in a star "hero" pin.

Plate 7

Clockwise from top left. ■ Fabric scraps are stitched with gold metallic thread. ■ Necklace combines favorite colors of cords, Ultrasuede strips, beads, and ribbon thread. ■ Eye cutouts from a magazine ad are glued to squares of needlework mounting board, covered with casting resin finish to make earrings *(see also far left)*. ■ Hand-embroidered pendant and tassel, hung with monk's cord. ■ Neckpiece, beaded by hand on Ultrasuede; "beauty pin" adjusts length. ■ Twisted cord and fabric, spiralled and glued to earring backs. ■ Cut hooks off fishing flies for instant earrings.

Plate 8

Clockwise from 11 o'clock. ■ Artist **dj Bennett** stitched glitzy fabric between Ultrasuede and tulle. ■ Frames of handmade paper sandwich a grid of thread. ■ Artist **Joy Clucas** of Colchester, England, machine stitches sequins and beads to hoops *(see Joy's earrings at center also)*. ■ Artist **Jackie Fischer** of Palatine, Ill., combines fabric and paint to create stunning jewelry. ■ Artist **Jane Elkins** of Hinsdale, Ill., strings wallpaper beads on velvet ribbon. ■ Artist **Joy Clucas** machine embroidered gold metallic thread leaves.

Project 9: Twisted satin stitches

3.4 *Twisted satin stitch showing heavy bobbin thread*

3.5 *Twisted satin stitched necklace*

Jane Warnick of Houston, TX, sent me the following cord idea, which stitches up fast on your sewing machine and is gorgeous. To make the cord, satin stitches cover a filler cord; then the stitches are twisted later to create a spiral of color.

Supplies needed:
Thread: (choose one) thick or thin gold metallic; gold braid; gold ribbon floss for bobbin; one hank six-strand embroidery floss for core; blue rayon machine embroidery thread

Miscellaneous: two cones; two jump rings; clasp set

Wind gold thread onto the bobbin: I've used metallic sewing threads, Madeira's gold braid, and ribbon floss. Each gives its own unusual effect so try each of them. (Remember, with a thick bobbin thread, a looser tension might be necessary to keep the bobbin feeding smoothly.)

Choose the top thread color to match the filler or core you stitch over to make this cord. I used blue, shiny rayon machine-embroidery thread (Sulky) in the needle, and blue embroidery floss for the core.

Take the presser foot off and put it aside. Lower or cover the feed dogs if possible.

Pull out the end of the hank from a skein of six-strand embroidery floss and determine the length of cord you want. Add a couple of inches for an overhand knot and cut eight lengths. Tie an overhand knot to hold the lengths together at one end with the thumb and index fingers of your left hand.

Slide the knot behind the needle. Hold the cord ends together in front of the needle at the base of the needle plate with your other hand. Set stitch width on 5, or the widest stitch that will clear the filler cord. Satin stitch over the thick core of embroidery floss (or try other cores). Whatever you use, when you sew, the satin stitches must be close together and create a tight stitch.

Move the core slowly as you stitch over it. If you use fine thread in the bobbin, you are able to pull the core under the needle more slowly than if you use something like ribbon floss in the bobbin. Thick bobbin threads build up quickly and pulling too slowly may knot up the bobbin area. (This is why the core and top thread colors must be the same. When using thicker threads, you must pull the cord faster, which means the stitches are farther

apart and the core visible in places.)

Adjust the top tension, if necessary, so the bobbin thread is seen. Play with the tensions. By loosening the bobbin and tightening the top slightly, the thicker threads seem to bubble around the core, my favorite result.

When stitching is completed, go back and twist the stitches around the core for an interesting effect. The cord is stiff. Use it as is for the necklace, finishing the ends as shown on page 62; or braid it with other cords, or twist and wrap it back on itself for a monk's cord and twist it into earrings.

Instant Idea

3. *Loop a piece of fine cord through an earring finding and spread glue on the cord. Press three worry dolls onto the cord to make an instant earring.*

Project 10: Worry doll necklace

3.6 *Worry doll necklace*

Here is another idea for satin stitching cords. This time the core isn't covered completely; the satin stitching is used to add color and hold the core threads together at intervals.

I made this necklace (see Color Plate 1) from lengths of threads and tiny Guatemalan worry dolls, which I purchased at a craft store.

Traditionally, the little handmade dolls (also called trouble dolls) are given to Guatemalan children by their parents. Whenever the child has a worry, she is to share it with her doll. By sharing the worry, it disappears. Usually the dolls come six to a box, so a child is allowed only six worries or troubles in one day.

Supplies needed:
Stitch width: widest
Stitch length: 0
Tension: normal
Needle: #90/14
Feed dogs: covered or lowered
Presser foot: none
Thread: teal blue, red, bright yellow, fuchsia, and purple rayon machine embroidery; 36"-long (90cm-long) strands of multicolored threads or three hanks of six-strand embroidery floss
Accessories: several packages of worry dolls (available at craft stores)
Stabilizer: water-soluble (optional)

Embroidery floss comes in hanks, which you can open into large loops and stitch into a necklace. I found it easier to cut the loops and work with lengths instead of circles of threads.

If the cords you've chosen are not in a circle or hank to begin with, first measure the length of the necklace you want to make and add 4" (10cm) more for the join. My necklace of many dozens of threads laid side by side is 32" + 4" (82cm + 10cm). Before stitching them, I stranded (pulled apart) all the threads to make a plumper necklace.

Use water-soluble stabilizer under the threads if necessary with your machine. Set up your machine for free machining and take off the presser foot. Place your left hand behind the needle, right hand at the front with pearl cotton cords taut between them (don't try to stitch over more than you can handle easily). The satin stitch must enclose the threads to give a smooth finish. Use the widest zigzag and satin stitch for about 2" (5cm) or 3" (8cm) and back again to cover the cords. You control the length of the stitches; keep them close together so you don't see any pearl cotton between them. Stitch several areas of satin stitches with the same color. I stitch one area then, without cutting the thread, pull it from the needle and bobbin to the next place I want to stitch and so

3.7 *Satin stitch over cord, pull down to another spot to satin stitch, and hold cords together.*

on. Then I have few starts and stops and it adds color to my necklace. Change to another

color and go on stitching threads together. Go back and join threads as

3.8 *Join two sections together with satin stitches.*

shown. Continue holding cords together and satin stitching over them until the necklace is completed to your satisfaction.

Overlap and place the ends next to each other. Satin stitch over the join, then clip the ends back to the join. You may

3.9 *Place cords side by side and satin stitch over them.*

want to join the necklace a few threads at a time so it looks more like the rest of the necklace.

Another possibility for joining is to create a tassel at center front of the necklace by tying and wrapping all the cords together.

3.10 *Join cords together to make a tassel.*

Determine where the center back is. Flatten the threads and hold them horizontally. Straight stitch up and back across all the threads to hold the necklace together at center back. This helps keep the threads from tangling later.

Dot the beginnings and ends of satin stitches with Fray Check. Add worry dolls, stitching them by hand to the tops of the satin stitches.

Other possibilities are to string beads on the cords before satin stitching them, or to add decorative buttons or clay or wooden animals, fruit, or flowers.

3.11 *Satin stitch over cord strung with beads, pull thread down past bead, then satin stitch to keep bead in place.*

Project 11: Gold and pearls stickpin

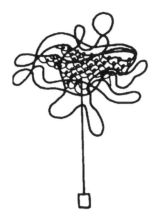

3.12 *Gold and pearls stickpin*

Here is another project using satin stitches and your sewing machine. Use this free-form idea for a stickpin (see Color Plate 12), but you can adapt it to earrings, too.

Supplies needed:
Thread: gold metallic machine embroidery thread for top and bobbin

Miscellaneous: 24" (61cm) covered florist's wire (available at craft stores); five freshwater pearls; one stick pin finding; hand sewing needle

Lower the feed dogs on your machine and stitch without a presser foot, or use a cording foot on the machine and set the machine on stitch width 3 and a satin stitch length that will cover the wire, yet lets the wire travel through the foot evenly.

When completely covered, bend the wire into shape by scrunching it up, then pulling it back into a pleasant shape.

Thread up your hand-sewing needle with gold metallic thread. Stitch needle lace by buttonholing across the empty spaces you've chosen to cover. Then place the pearls where you wish. If

3.13 *Buttonhole stitch by hand to needle lace in space.*

they are beads, use the holes to stitch them to the pin, but if this isn't possible, then use glue (I used 527) to keep them in place.

Making cords from filled tubes

Tubes are the most versatile cords you can make or buy. Purchased Fabric Cord is available by the yard or roll.

It comes in many popular colors, prints, or plain muslin. Plain colors are wonderful backgrounds for dye, fabric paint, or markers. Knot Fabric Cord, wrap it with lustrous pearl cotton, slip beads on or dangle things from it.

Or create elegant silk tubes with fabric left from garment sewing. Make several spaghetti cords to knot or braid together.

But men's ties are my choice when I want to make tubes from scratch. They are cut on the bias, and drape beautifully. Leave them as is, or embellish them with hand or machine embroidery before making the tube.

Tubes from ties

I suggest using men's ties because not only are they already on the bias, but often they are a source of beautiful silk, with patterns and stripes you can decoratively stitch with automatic stitches.

To use a tie, first cut it apart and take out all the inside stabilizers (put those aside—someday we'll come up with a use for them). Press the tie open.

Determine how wide you want the tube and mark it on the tie. Front sides together, fold the tie in half the long way, but don't press it unless a pressing line will not show on your finished project. Stitch the tube and turn it. For closures, use Velcro dots (if tubes are wide enough), or snaps; if the finished necklace is long enough, cut back each cord on one side, slip one end into the other, and stitch by hand to make a continuous circle.

3.14 Cut cord back inside, then slip one side of the outer covering over the other side, turn under the edge and hand stitch in place.

As an alternative or an addition to men's ties, buy Fabric Cord at a fabric store or make bias-cut tubes, then fill them yourself, if needed, with acrylic yarn, cable cord, or light batting to knot or bead. You can also shape the tubes by cutting out a pattern using a commercial collar pattern.

Use the following ideas for those finished tubes:

Tube and decorative knots

Fill the tube with cable cord or an acrylic yarn. Knot the center using a decorative knot, such as the Josephine knot.

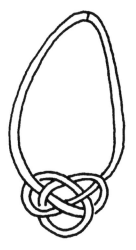

3.15 *Tie tube into a decorative knot, such a the Josephine.*

Beads and knots

Do you have smashing beads you've been saving for something special? Find the center of the tube and work from one side to another, adding beads and knotting between (see Color Plate 4). That's all there is to

it. This tube is better not filled with cord, but if you wish, you can use something lightweight.

3.16 *Make tube from man's tie and knot on favorite beads.*

Fill the tube with cable cord. Find the center and loop it over a metal or glass bead disk as shown (see Color Plate 5).

3.17 *Knot a brass disk in the center of a tube necklace.*

Instant Ideas

4. *Fold under both sides of a piece of lamé. Stitch gold threads on lamé (as above), then fold it over to make tassel top. Optional: Add more threads up inside before wrapping under the fabric to make the tassel top.*

5. *Satin stitch over jute for free-form necklace. Add beads by slipping them on to the jute core first, then satin stitching to the beads and after them to hold them in place.*

Instant Ideas

6. *Cover a cord with a tube twice as long as the cord. This makes a gathered cord, an alternative to smooth covers.*

7. *Make nine long strings of beads, then braid them together and create a beaded tassel for each end. Wear this braid as a necklace by looping the braid and letting the tassels hang in front.*

Project 12: Beads in tube necklace

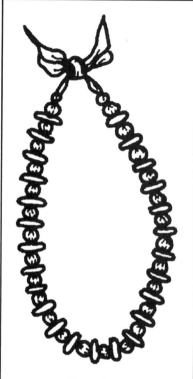

3.18 *Beads in tube necklace*

(See Color Plate 3.)

Supplies needed:
Fabric: 3"-wide (8cm-wide) silk strip at least 45" long (1.1m long)
Beads: 30 (size, 6mm) round beads (these are hidden, so I use all the lightweight, junky ones I don't want anymore); 31 (size 12mm x 5mm) rondelles in a color to blend, contrast, or match the tube

Fold the silk strips in half the long way (right sides together). Stitch the tube, beginning by stitching from a point. Leave the other end open. Turn the tube to the right side.

Make an overhand knot 8" (21cm) from the closed point. With a fine crochet hook, slip the hook through a rondelle bead (be sure the center hole is large enough) and catch hold of the end of the tube. Pull the tube through the rondelle and seat it next to the knot.

Now slip a round bead into the tube, string another rondelle bead, add another bead inside the tube and repeat until almost 8" (21cm) from the open end. Make another overhand knot to hold the last bead in place inside the tube. Cut the end of the tube to a point, turn edges under and stitch in place by hand.

This tube necklace (see Color Plate 16) is

3.19 *Fold fabric, right sides together, and stitch across end and down one side. Turn to right side.*

3.20 *Pull tube through beads with a crochet hook.*

3.21 *Knot first, then slip bead into the tube, string on rondelle bead, slip another bead inside, string rondelle bead outside, and continue until completed.*

3.22 *Beads and knots necklace*

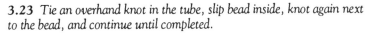

3.23 *Tie an overhand knot in the tube, slip bead inside, knot again next to the bead, and continue until completed.*

much the same as the previous one, but the tube must be much longer because overhand knots eat up fabric. It's best to do a sample first.

Instead of adding rondelles between beads, tie overhand knots in between. To knot close to the bead, tie a loose overhand knot close to the bead. Then place a long needle down inside the knot, pull up on the

3.24 *Place point of needle in knot center and snug up knot to bead.*

tube, working the knot down tight to the bead.

Or instead of knots, use wrappings of gold cord or wire; or a jump ring or washer between beads for a different look.

Tie the ends of the tube to fasten. If you piece wider strips at the ends of the necklace, the bows are more full and decorative. Wear the bow to the side, in front, or in back.

Tubes from collars

Project 13: Suede tube neckpiece with Sculpey pin

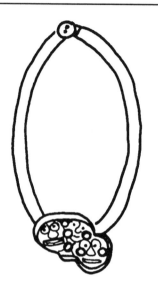

3.25 *Collar neckpiece with Sculpey pin*

Have you noticed that sometimes tube necklaces encircle your neck like a circle of sausage? I found a way to construct a tube necklace so it hugs your neck at both sides (see Color Plate 1).

Supplies needed:
Fabric: suede or suedelike piece 12" x 18" (31cm x 46cm) (depends on size of tube)
Thread: polyester sewing thread to match suede
Miscellaneous: commercial collar pattern, scrap of fabric collar size, fiberfill (enough to stuff neck piece), 3" (8cm) of monk's cord, 5/8" (16mm) button, hand-sewing needle and thread, Sculpey pin (optional)

Draw the collar on a piece of paper, using the commercial collar pattern, then draw the shape and size of the tube you wish to construct, letting

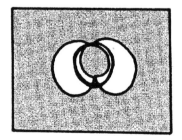

3.26 *Draw a pattern for a tube that hugs the neck.*

it hug the neck edge. Fold the pattern in half and cut out the tube shape, using one side as the pattern—this way both halves will be the same. Discard the rest of the paper. Try on the paper pattern before cutting it from fabric. Then add 1/4" (6mm) seam allowances.

3.27 *Fold pattern in half and cut so sides are the same. Double check shape by trying on pattern before cutting it out of fabric.*

I stitch right sides together, leaving an area in the front seam opening for turning. This is hidden once my beads and buttons are sewn in place. I stuff the tube with fiberfill, but use little filling in the last 2" (5cm) of the back closure area. The collarbone area also is not filled tight—I'm able to flatten it a bit, which I think looks better than the round, sausage look.

One end of the back is folded under and stitched. Then I run a monk's cord through the loop I've made to loop over the button sewn to the other side. See Color Plate 1.

3.28 *Monk's cord loop and button closure*

I attach a Sculpey pin to the center front, which I can remove from the necklace when I want to wear the pin separately or add something else to the necklace.

Manipulating threads and fabric

Next, cover Fabric Cord with yarn or thread, then take out your knitting frame or your spool and nails to knit idiot cord. Learn to make monk's cord with your sewing machine, two pencils, or a hand drill. What choices! Following that, travel back to the 1960s and make a rick-rack cord necklace. Incorporate your original beads in or on your cords.

Instant Ideas

8. *Cut rick-rack into lengths to make a belt. Use a dozen pieces of rick-rack—many colors and widths. Use tassel wrapping to hold the rick-rack together 6" (15cm) from each end and in the center back. Tie on beads, clay animals, and charms, or tie the rick-rack into knots at the ends to finish.*

Project 14: Pearl cotton necklace

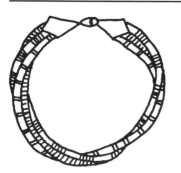

3.29 Pearl cotton wrapped necklace

I can think of several reasons for making this necklace (see Color Plate 9); you need an exact color match for a garment; you are a stitcher and want to get rid of pearl cotton leftovers; or you would like to give a special gift to a friend.

Supplies needed:

Cord and Thread: #5 or #3 (these can be combined) pearl cotton in several colors; 2 yds. (1.8m) of Fabric Cord cut into 3 equal pieces (available in fabric stores—see text); polyester thread

Miscellaneous: cones plus closures for ends of necklaces; hand-sewing needle; scissors; water-erasable or vanishing marker

First choose pearl cotton colors. Combining #5 (medium thickness) and #3 (thick) pearl cottons is acceptable, but combining #3 (thick) with #8 (fine) shows too much contrast. If you choose #8, then wrap consistently with that size or use it with #5.

An excellent reason for using thicker threads is that the wrapping goes faster. Of course you can wrap with other types of threads, yarns, cords, and combinations of them, but I chose pearl cotton because the color palette seems all-inclusive, and the lustrous sheen of pearl cotton is beautiful.

After finding colors to use, cut fabric-covered cord into three 24" (61cm) lengths. Fabric Cord is available at fabric shops and through mail order. It's available by the yard or by the spool. It's used for belt making and crafts and it comes in several sizes, colors, and prints. It is sturdy, filled cotton tubing. I chose muslin color, but if I were to do a neck piece with dark colors predominating, I'd choose a darker cord.

I used the narrow 1/4" (6mm) size. (The size is not on the spool, but I flattened the cord on top of my ruler and it covered a space 1/4" [6mm] wide.) Cut off the length you need.

Fabric Cord is sturdier than cable cord (which can also be used), and I think wrapping it is easier and more even. But, yes, you can substitute cable cord or even heavy maxi-cord or macramé jute.

If you prefer joining the ends so the necklace can be slipped over your head, then wrap it around your head first to measure the length, adding enough extra cord to allow you to slip it on and off.

Allow at least 3" (7.5cm) extra, for over-lapping the ends (2" [5cm] at one end, 1" [2.5cm] on the opposite end). This is important to know later for the marker lines you draw on the tube for starting and stopping.

Plan your color placement before you begin. If you plan to use cones at the ends, leave at least 1" (2.5cm) free of wraps at each end of the Fabric Cord. Draw a line with a water-erasable or vanishing marker at these two places. Then, with a ruler, mark off areas for the colors you'll use. If

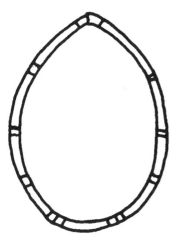

3.30 Mark with ruler for colors and 1" (2.5cm) from end for cones.

you wish, write the names of the colors in the sections on the fabric cord. If you plan to

change colors throughout your wrapping without worrying about consistency, then forego all marks except those at the ends.

Always begin a color by laying a loop of the thread on the fabric cord, extending the loop 1" (2.5cm) from the line you've marked, with its end facing the direction

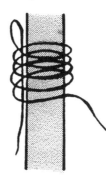

3.31 Lay pearl cotton next to Fabric Cord, then wrap over it to anchor the thread.

you'll wrap. Hold the thread down at the place you'll begin and start wrapping over the thread to secure it. Wrap snuggly and close to, but not overlapping, the previous wrap. That's all there is to it.

To change colors, leave about an inch of cord from the previous color, begin the second the same way you did the first, but this time wrap over both threads. This

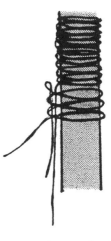

3.32 To change color, leave several inches of pearl cotton to wrap over. Start another piece of pearl as you did the first time.

holds the first thread in place without having to sew it down or glue it, and also holds down the second color. When you've reached the end of the Fabric Cord, loop the thread around one last time, but draw the cord end through the loop to keep it in place until you can complete the other cords, or until you can complete the closures.

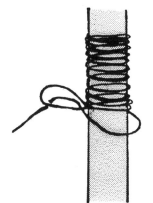

3.33 *Tie an overhand knot when finished to hold pearl cotton in place.*

If you are overlapping the ends for a necklace that slips over your head, then on one end cut filling and covering on a slant. On the other end, open the seam for 2" (5cm) and cut back the filling 1/2" (1.3cm) on a slant. Slip the first side inside the second end (here's where you may want a dot of glue stick to help hold it in place) and pull the fabric covering over the inserted cord.

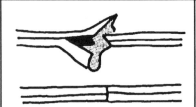

3.34 *Clip seam open and cut filling on slant. Cut other end on slant and slip into first side. Glue to hold.*

Glue sparingly under the fabric to hold it in place until you wrap that section with pearl cotton. By cutting the cords on a slant, even though they're too fuzzy to fit one slant on top of the other exactly, you're eliminating much of the bulk so the two ends combine smoothly. With the fabric drawn over the join, it is wrapped smoothly and the join becomes almost invisible. If you plan to add a decoration, such as a decorative pin or button, then add it over the join and wear that at center front.

To finish the ends with cones, find two that are large enough in which to fit the tubes.

First stitch the three tubes together, side by

side, leaving a long thread free. Next, slip the cones on each side, pulling the thread out the end, around the lobster claw closure or around jump rings first and then back to anchor in the cords. If you've attached jump rings first then, after the thread is anchored, spread apart the jump rings and slip the lobster claw closure on the rings. Close the rings.

Twisting monk's cord

The most useful cord is monk's cord. It's made from several strands of thread or yarn held together and twisted to make a thick cord. The cord may be used in many ways—as a finish around pillows, as a handle for handbags, or as a thick fringe in tassels, passementerie button loops, and necklace cords.

On the machine, monk's cord is made using the bobbin winder and a cord such as #8 pearl cotton. (If it is too thick, it will not seat properly on the winder, so the size you can use is limited.) However, there is a way to get around this. You can tie dental floss—it doesn't slip—around the center of a thick cord, leaving long enough ends to seat the floss into the middle of the bobbin. Then you are able to wind monk's cord of any thickness.

Start with a length of pearl cotton about 2 yards (1.8m) long. Fold this in half, knot the two ends together, and slip the knot down through the center of a bobbin. Let an inch or two (2.5–5cm) of cord extend beyond the bobbin.

Next, push the bobbin down into place on the pin. When clicked into

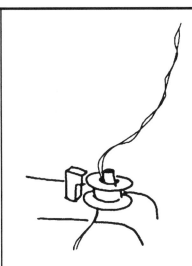

3.35 *Place cord inside bobbin and seat on spindle.*

place, the bobbin will hold the cord securely. Put your index finger or a pencil in the loop of the cord at the other end and stand over the bobbin mechanism, stretching the cord upward to keep tension on it. Activate the bobbin mechanism. Working with a partner helps. After you have the cord seated, put your index finger in the loop, hold onto the cord with your other hand, about 12" (30.5cm) from the bobbin. Stretch the cord to keep tension on it for this 12" (30.5cm). Click the mechanism to start

the bobbin with the hand that is holding the end of the cord. As soon as it starts to wind, let go with the hand closest to the bobbin, but keep the cord taut with the other hand by moving back away from the machine.

Keep winding the cord until it is so tight the blood supply to your finger is threatened. If you've used a pencil in the loop, how can you tell if the cord is wound tightly enough? Stop winding, but keep tension on the cord. Take hold of the cord about 6" (15cm) from the pencil. Don't let loose of the entire cord, only the 6" (15cm) between hand and pencil to see if it will twist tightly. If it does, then take the pencil out of the loop, find the middle of the cord with your free hand and, still keeping tension on the cord, place the loop on the spool pin. Don't let go of the cord, but from the end, work down the twists with both hands to keep the cord smooth.

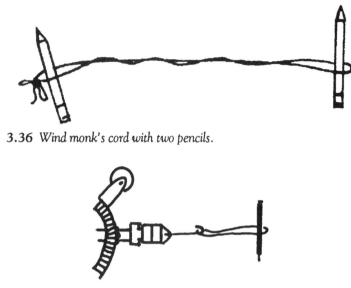

3.36 *Wind monk's cord with two pencils.*

3.37 *Use a hand drill to wind monk's cord fast.*

When it is twisted as tightly as it will go, take it out of the bobbin and off the thread holder spool pin. Tie an overhand knot to hold the two ends together until you actually use it. (Yes, you really need three hands.)

You don't need a sewing machine to make monk's cord, but working with a partner is a plus. One day my friend, Marilyn, and I made yards of monk's cords—trying different cords and yarns. We could have tied a pencil at each end and then each of us twisted in the opposite direction to make a cord, but we opted to use a hand drill. We substituted a long nail (which we bent into a hook; or use a cuphook) for the drill bit. The cord was doubled and tied in a knot at the end. We looped the cord over the hook, and I held on to the other end of the cord by looping it over my finger. Marilyn walked to the opposite end of the long room and began winding the cord. We made extremely long

cords this way. Each end was knotted when we finished so they wouldn't untwist. We cut several inches from each cord and made samples to keep above our sewing machines. Each cord was pinned to a card with the type of cord and number of strands used for each sample.

Knitting idiot cord

Many women I know once owned a wooden spool with four nails hammered into it, from which knitted cord was born. My father made me

3.38 *Spool, nails, pick, and yarn can make idiot cord.*

one and I'd love to say I made miles of cord, but it was so boring I could never stick with it. Once I had knit enough rounds to see my variegated yarn go through all the color changes, I quit. I didn't know what I'd do with the cord later anyway; my mother did not need another hot pad and it might have taken me 12 years to make a round purse; the only other thing I could think of making. Years later I learned that this cord is called idiot cord. What a fitting name for it (or for those who make it?).

Why am I adding it to this book? Because I'm older and wiser and I have a knitting frame. Don't despair if you don't have one of those. Idiot cord is made on knitting needles too. Directions for both follow.

Why would you want to make this cord (I assume you don't need a pot holder either)? Use it for jewelry, of course, but when made with yarn, it is also a gorgeous finish for sweaters or pillows (glitzy, furry, designer yarns add eye-appeal).

The tube is formed by knitting on double-pointed needles) in only one direction. By that I

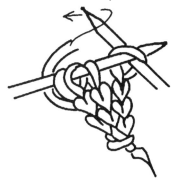

3.39 *Knit in one direction only on double pointed needles to make idiot cord.*

mean, after casting on four stitches (or whatever number you wish to use), knit the stitches off, and instead of turning your work and purling on the return, slip the stitches to the other end of the needle and knit them again. Pull up on the thread for the first stitch in each row so the first and last stitches are pulled together to form a tube (do you see how this imitates the spool and nails?).

It's not necessary to fill the tube later with cable cord, but if the needles are large enough to leave

openings with every stitch, then experiment and fill the tube with colored cord or rolled strips of colored fabrics. Once you've learned the technique, try different knitting yarns, sew beads on, or string the tube through beads.

If you have a knitting machine, you can make idiot cord even faster. My first experiment on the knitting machine was a success, thanks to Lois Christensen of Brookfield, IL. Lois is a knitting teacher and she agreed to show me how to knit idiot cord.

I used the following directions to make several yards of velour idiot cord before I quit, and must admit it beats the old spool and nails, though the results are the same.

I have a basic baby lock knitting frame and used key plate 3, chenille (velour) yarn (which looks like velvet), and only four stitches. I quickly knit two yards of tubing.

To do this, I cast ("e" wrap) on my stitches, then knit off one row (the carriage is now on the right). Next, I put all the needles in a holding position and moved the carriage back to the left without knitting.

I knit another row and kept knitting like this—in one direction—until the cord was the length I planned. The yarn closed up the edges to create a cord.

To make the necklace (see Color Plate 4), I cut off part of the cord (about 1-1/2 yds. [1.4m]), doubled it, and knotted it inside a large, long Sculpey bead (the knot is glued inside the bead with a dot of Goop), using the same clay left from my necklace and earrings (Chapter 2).

You can decorate yours differently by adding beads to the cord, or hanging a pendant from it. Combine pencil-slim cords with single strands of yarn and leathers, or simply make three tubes and braid them together.

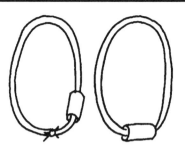

3.40 *String bead on idiot cord, knot cord, then hide knot inside of bead.*

Afterthought: If you stockinette stitch with only a few stitches, that will curl, too, but you must sew the edges together.

Stitching rick-rack

Project 15: Rick-rack necklace

(See Color Plate 10.)

If you've never seen one of these necklaces before, you may not recognize it as rick-rack. Use the cord alone without embellishment, but before you attach the two ends, tie a loose, overhand knot in the center front.

Look at the illustrations, then read the directions and refer to the illustrations again. It is much easier following the drawings than it is the written word.

Supplies needed:
Rick-rack: 3/8" white rayon (if you can find rayon) rick-rack (I used 20 yards [18m].) Buy rick-rack in one piece as the join isn't attractive (see Sources of Supplies).
Thread: white polyester sewing thread—36" (.9m) doubled, hand-sewing needle

Begin by knotting the sewing thread and stitching in the rick-rack several inches at the end. As you proceed to make the cord, always take two stitches at one time.

3.41 *Take two stitches at a time to make rick-rack cord.*

Don't try to load more than that onto the needle—it takes longer in the long run. Every time you stitch two stitches, twist the rick-rack so the folds lay neatly in place.

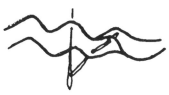

3.42 *Pull up thread after two stitches, to fold the rick-rack.*

3.43 *Each layer has five folds.*

There are five folds per layer.

3.44 *The cord will spiral.*

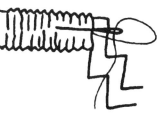

3.45 *If you run out of thread before finishing the cord, leave several inches of thread and stitch back in several folds.*

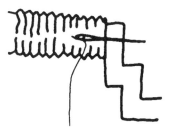

3.46 *Stitch back out again and anchor the thread.*

Before you get to the end of the thread (be sure you have several inches of thread left), poke out at the middle of the cord, turn your needle, and poke back through several layers. Pull tight. Turn again and stitch back to the end. Anchor the thread by stitching several times in one place.

Prepare the next thread as before, knotting the end. Poke in where your anchor stitches are, stitch through several layers, then back out again. Go on stitching

3.47 *Start a new thread by tying a knot in the thread, then stitching in through the anchor and through several folds.*

3.48 *Stitch back out again at the same spot.*

and drawing up the rick-rack folds till you reach the end of the thread again, or finish the length of cord you want.

To join two pieces of rick-rack—if the pieces are too short for an entire necklace—first use Fray Check on the cut edges you want to join. When dry, ladder stitch the ends together and continue.

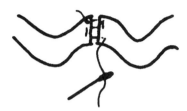

3.49 *To join two pieces of rick-rack, dot edges with Fray Check and use the ladder stitch to hold them together.*

When the length is completed, stitch to anchor, but don't cut the thread yet. Then tie an overhand knot in the cord, at center front, before joining the cord.

Fit the two rick-rack ends together (you will clip off the tail at the beginning of the necklace to fit the last fold so the necklace folds are consistent) and stitch together by sewing from one side

3.50 *Tie an overhand knot before stitching the join.*

(using the thread you didn't cut at the end) to the other—through several folds—and back again. Anchor and cut off the thread. Place a dot of glue on the anchor.

3.51 *To combine ends, stitch into the other side, through several folds, then back out again. Pull tight.*

After making the necklace, I made rick-rack flower earrings—oh, very 1960s—from the same hank of rick-rack (see Chapter 5).

3.52 *Stitch into anchor at the other side, then pull tight and finish off by anchoring again.*

We haven't exhausted the subject of cords, but you've learned enough to make all the projects in this book. I've used all these techniques on the jewelry that follows.

In the next chapter you'll learn how to hold your jewelry together with either commercial metal clasps or with closures for fabric pieces, which you can find at the notions counter in a fabric store.

4. Clasps and Closures

Once I started accumulating methods for finishing jewelry, I found such diverse methods, as well as differences within the same methods, that almost anything goes. Once you begin making jewelry, you'll be like me and use only the ones you're comfortable with (and probably invent a few more). But the following will get you started thinking about clasps and closures.

Plan the clasp or closure you need before beginning a piece of jewelry. To tell the truth, I'm always happier when I can slip a necklace over my head without using a closure, or can fashion a bracelet without a clasp, but most of the time closures are necessary. Be certain the one you make or choose is appropriate to the rest of your necklace or bracelet: I wouldn't use a gold, ornate cone and clasp with painted muslin necklaces. You can buy or make closures. Don't forget to save and use the clasps from necklaces you take apart to make other jewelry. When you make closures, try to eliminate bulk.

Attaching commercial clasps

Lobster claws and spring clasps are sometimes available at notions counters, but usually you'll find them at craft shops, or look in Sources of Supplies.

When a necklace is finished, except for a closure, I usually add a jump ring to each end before attaching the clasp. Once sewn in place, the jump rings are twisted open and the clasps slipped onto them. Then twist the jump rings closed again. Although not always necessary, adding jump rings makes the clasp and necklace join less rigid so it is easier to put the necklace on and take it off.

Tiger tail and crimp beads

When making heavy necklaces or those with beads that may cut fiber cord, string the beads with plastic-covered wire (tiger tail), then use a crimp bead at the closure. To use one, first insert the tiger tail through the bead, then the clasp or jump ring, and back through the bead again.

4.1 Push tiger tail (plastic covered wire) through a crimp bead, into a clasp or jump ring, and back through the bead. Crush the bead to hold the cord in place.

Pull on the cord to hold the clasp close to the bead, then crunch the bead with pliers, and string the tiger tail through several beads at each side of the necklace before you cut it off.

4.2 String cord back through several beads and clip off.

Crimp beads may cut fiber bead cords so they aren't used on those fibers.

Bead tips and fiber cords

Use knot covers (bead tips) to hide the end knots when using fiber cords. The cord is slipped into the hole, and a knot is tied and dotted with glue, cement, or clear fingernail polish. Then the end of the cord is clipped back and the cover is closed. A jump

4.3 Slip cord into a bead tip, knot the cord, and dot with glue.

ring or clasp is introduced into the hook and the hook of the bead tip is bent over it.

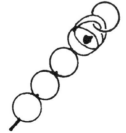

4.4 Slip jump ring on a bead tip and bend top over the ring.

Tape and eye pin

When a necklace is made up of several soft cords, first find the center of the necklace and pin it at the center on a board. (I work on a smocking board, but ceiling tile works well, too.) Pull down the cords at both sides. Stroke through them until they are straight. At this point you can slip cord through an eye pin at both ends. Push above ends. Then, completing one side at a time, grasp the end of the cords firmly to hold them together, wrap them tightly with thread (see Fig. 4.6) and tie off.

4.5 Stroke yarn so it hangs correctly when you wear it.

4.6 *Tie off both ends of the necklace.*

Finish both sides. Go back and wrap ends with thread or duct or masking tape. Cut off any cord beyond the tape or wrap. Now your necklace will hang straight. If you were to lay the cords straight out at each side and wrap them, you wouldn't be satisfied because of the unevenness of the necklace when you wore it.

Grasp the necklace ends. Push the eye pin up through the center of the cords.

4.7 *Slip yarn through eye pin before taping ends.*

If you didn't add the eye pin before tying the cords together, then push an eye pin up through the center of the cords now. Stitch from one side to the other through the eye pin to hold it in place.

4.8 *An alternative method is to stitch eye pin in place.*

Now coat the tape or thread wraps with a thin layer of glue, and with a piece of yarn or soft cord from the necklace, wrap around the tape or thread to hide it, if necessary, or to keep the cords snug in the cone. Then slip the eye pin through a cone on each side of the

4.9 *Push the eye pin up through the cone.*

necklace. Bend the straight ends over jump rings (use needle-nosed pliers). Then add the clasps.

4.10 *Bend the eye pin over a jump ring.*

Knot and eye pin

You can use the next method if you leave enough cord at both ends of the necklace to tie an overhand knot. Under the knot at each end, push an eye pin (stitching through the eye part to attach it securely to the knot, or slip necklace

4.11 *Knot both ends of necklace and push eye pins through the knots; then stitch them to the cords.*

cords through the eye pin before tying the knot). On both sides slip the eye pin through the hole in the cone, place a jump

4.12 *Push the eye pin up through the cone.*

ring on it, then bend the end of the eye pin over (use needle-nosed pliers) to hold the ring in place. Then finish by attaching a clasp.

4.13 *Bend the eye pin over a jump ring.*

To finish either of these, when using many cords, I glue up into the cords (inside the cones) to make sure that none of them eventually works free.

Instant Idea

1. *Wrap a jute cord by hand or satin stitch over it, leaving enough cord at the end to slip on a large bead, knot the cord, then dot with glue to hold it in place.*

At the other end, wrap or satin stitch over jute, then fold over a loop at the end, leaving enough space to slip in the bead to complete the closure. Then satin stitch or wrap the cord back on itself.

Project 16: Minestrone necklace

4.14 *Create a necklace with fluffy yarns, called Minestrone, tied into an overhand knot.*

This is one of the fastest necklaces anyone can make (see Color Plate 4). It's named after the yarn itself, Minestrone, which is so decorative, with slubs, furry things hanging off of it, and a variety of colors, that it needs no other embellishment. I used approximately half the hank, then cut through that half to attach clasps.

Supplies needed:
Yarn: hank of furry, slubby yarn (use 1/2 or more) or combine several kinds of yarn
Miscellaneous: two cones, clasp set, two eye pins, two jump rings, masking tape, craft glue, hand-sewing needle, and sewing thread (optional)

All you have to do is find the center of the yarn, tie an overhand knot, then pin it to a board and follow the directions above to attach clasps.

Using closures for soft surfaces

You can use Velcro, buttons, even snaps, or hooks and eyes for soft jewelry closures.

4.15 Velcro closure

Secure lightweight Velcro dots or squares by sewing. The side that overlaps on top is sewn through only the underside of the necklace so stitches aren't visible—or the stitches are hidden with a decorative button.

You can also use different sizes of snaps or hooks and eyes. I like the

4.16 Hook and bar closure

plastic snaps that are practically invisible when sewn in place. When I use hooks, I often eliminate the eye and stitch a thread bar across the end.

Decorative buttons or large beads with loops are useful, too.

4.17 Large beads and button loops closure

And if you use long ribbons or tubes for necklaces, you can use the old faithful bow as the closure.

4.18 Tie a bow closure

2. *Instead of making a pendant, finish two circles of embroidery, turn under at the edges, and leave out the cardboard, but add batting and lining (also turned under at the edge) and stitch each side separately by whipping or ladder stitching around the edges to hold lining to top. Then stitch the two sides together to make a tiny embroidered purse. Add a button and loop on top for a closure and monk's cord for hanging.*

Instant Idea

3. *To make a beaded closure: When the beading cord is wire, add enough extra beads to the wire to form a loop when bent back on itself. Wrap the end over itself between two beads. Make a hook on the other side by bending the end of the wire back on itself and into the last several beads. Bend into a hook to create a closure.*

Making adjustable closures

Sliding bead closure

4.19 *Adjustable bead closure*

Another common closure incorporates two cords strung through a large bead. If the cords are tight enough inside the bead, the necklace is adjustable.

Fisherman's knot closure

My favorite closure, because the length can be adjusted, uses two beads and is based on the fisherman's knot. Directions for pendants—and the adjustable cord— follow.

Project 17: Pins and pendants

4.20 *Pendant with adjustable cord*

These pins and pendants can be worked using free-machine embroidery, your machine's decorative stitches, or by hand embroidery (see Color Plate 14). Even if you use one of my designs, the outcome will be original. That's what I like about them: There are no two alike.

If you want to forego embroidery, then find a fabric you love and make a pin or pendant from it following the finishing instructions. Or use recycled fabrics (see Chapter 5).

These projects can be finished as large pins, buttons, earrings, or pendants. Cut any shape from cardboard, or buy button forms at fabric or needlecraft shops. I used size 75, which is about 2" (5cm) in diameter, for pins. Earrings need a

4.21 *Hand embroidered pendant*

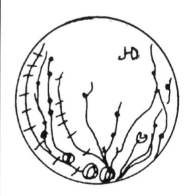

4.22 *Back of pendant*

smaller size. I was inspired by Mary Ann Spawn of Tacoma, WA, to finish some of them by attaching cords to make pendants (see Color Section).

Supplies needed:
Fabric suggestion: medium-weight, tightly woven linen; silky look polyesters
Thread: machine-embroidery thread; pearl cotton; embroidery floss
Accessories: wood or spring hoop (or freezer paper stabilizer for machine embroidery), button forms or cardboard, batting, craft glue, cord

If you use the round design, draw two circles with the same center point on your fabric. One is the area to be embroidered; the other circle, 1/2" (13mm) outside the first, is the cutting line. It's important to keep the area between the lines free from stitching. Use a piece of

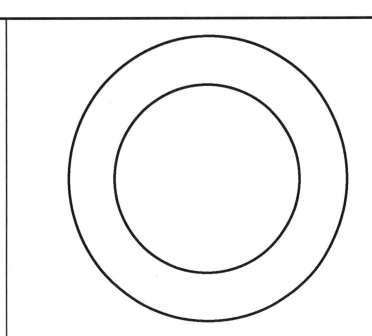

4.23 *Use this round design for a pendant.*

fabric large enough to go into a spring hoop if you embroider by machine (this is optional if done by hand); and place a piece of tear-away stabilizer underneath if stitched by machine. You can also use ironed-on freezer paper with no hoop or tear-away.

When stitching by machine, combine different widths of satin stitches and lines of straight stitches. Use small blobs of satin stitches connected by straight lines. Stitch blobs on top of each other for texture. Use your machine's decorative stitches, too, with

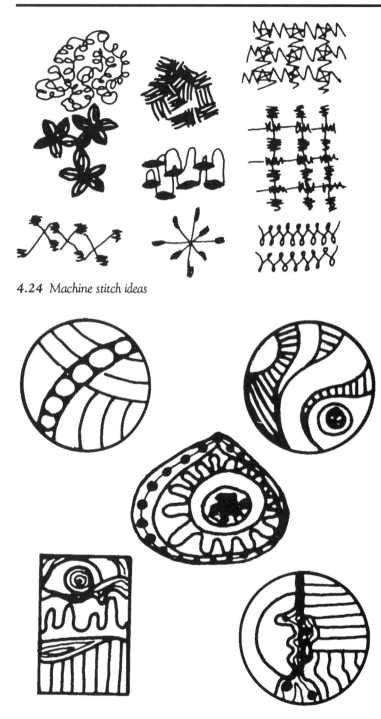

4.24 *Machine stitch ideas*

4.25 *Design ideas to enlarge and use*

free embroidery. Here is a chance to use your imagination.

Use shiny rayon embroidery threads or pearl cotton when you embroider by hand. Use my designs or your own. I think backs of pendants are as important as the fronts, and I always embroider a simple all-over design and sign the pendant there.

To finish the buttons or pendants, cut out the shapes. For buttons, use large button forms for the round ones and follow the directions on the button package. For pendants, place the embroidered piece on a piece of batting over the cardboard shape, both cut to the size of the inner circle. For the back, cut a piece of plain fabric the same size as the front (or use another embroidered piece you've done). Also cut batting and cardboard, as for the front. You can use two methods to assemble. For the first, use a dot of thick craft

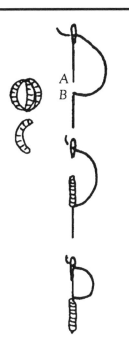

4.29 *Couch down thread with tiny stitches.*

4.32 *Sew running stitch around the edge of the pendant top.*

4.30 *Use this detached chain stitch for flower petals.*

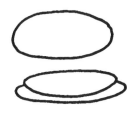

4.33 *Layer cardboard, batting, and pendant top.*

4.26 *Bullion knot: Needle in at A and point out at B. Wrap needle with thread and pull needle through wraps. Insert needle back at A.*

4.31 *Feather stitches make good flower stems and leaves.*

4.34 *Draw up the running stitches and anchor in place around the cardboard.*

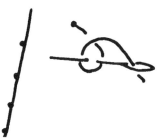

4.27 *Scroll stitch for flower stems and grasses.*

glue to hold the batting in place on the cardboard. Then run glue around the underside of the cardboard and stretch the embroidery over the top and press it down on the glue underneath. For

the second method, which I prefer, use a hand-running stitch at the edge of the pendant. Pull up on the thread to keep the batting and fabric in place around the

4.28 *Outline stitch for stems and outlines.*

cardboard shape. Then join the two pieces of cardboard, back to back, by dabbing glue between the cardboard pieces and whipping or ladder stitching around the edge by hand.

Measure a length of monk's cord (see Chapter 3), and tie an overhand knot at each end. Stitch the knots to the top or sides of the pendants by hand or slip the ends of the cord inside the two halves before stitching the two halves together.

Cover the edge with monk's cord if you like, or use beads, hand stitching them to the edge.

4.35 Cover the pendant edge with monk's cord.

The free ends of the pendants are pulled through two beads. If you look closely at it, you'll see that it imitates the fisherman's knot. In place of the knot, however, I've substituted two beads. No matter how long your cords, you can adjust them to fit your neckline.

4.36 Use a fisherman's knot adjustable closure for pendants.

4.37 Pendant pattern taken from silk fabric

Afterthought: One of my favorite pendants is hand embroidered on a silk print fabric (see Color Plate 5). I embellished the design in the fabric on both sides of the pendant. The cord and tassel were once a necklace I bought for ten cents at a garage sale. After separating the tassel from the chain, I stitched the tassel to the center front of the pendant and hung the chain necklace from the pendant.

4.38 Fine chain and beads tassled necklace

4.39 Cut apart and use cords and tassels on pendant.

Plate 9

Clockwise from top left. ■ Southwestern pin in Ultrasuede, feathers, beads, and quills. ■ Necklace made from pearl cotton wrapped over fabric cord. ■ Indian doll pin: beads, quills, charms and buttons. ■ Antler button pin, decorated with beads, quills, suede strips, copper and beads. ■ Ready-made suede barrette with copper, beads, quills added. ■ Chamois tube necklace, adjustable bead closure. ■ Stretch Ultrasuede around cardboard shape and decorate with suede strips, beads, quills, and feathers.

Plate 10

Clockwise from top left. ■ Machine-embroidered lace, recycled into a beaded barrette. ■ Buttons glued on earring findings. ■ Bracelet of buttons, sewn to double-crocheted elastic cord. ■ Lace earrings stitched on stabilizer. ■ Gathered tube with Velcro closure. ■ Rick-rack rose used as pin or shoe clip. ■ Instant earrings of ready-made stars glued on findings. ■ Folds of rick-rack sewn together to make a necklace. ■ Rick-rack interlocked and spiralled into earrings.

Plate 11

Top to bottom. ■ Use a leather punch to make a suede lace scarf. ■ Indian medicine necklace. ■ Indian doll pins, decorated with fur, beads, quills, feathers.

Plate 12
Clockwise from top center. ■ Sampler of cords made by serger and sewing machine. ■ "Stained glass earrings" made with transparent fabric scraps. ■ Earrings stitched with metallic thread on stabilizer (*see also top left corner*). ■ Recycle embroideries to make heart-shaped beaded pins. ■ Earrings are both greeting card and gift! ■ Wire stick pin, hand and machine stitches.

Making a loop closure

Instead of sewing or knotting on a clasp, fold under and stitch the end of a scarf to create a loop. Thread the other end through this channel, then pull up to adjust it.

Project 18: Suede scarf

4.40 *Use scarf clip (or barrette) to hold ends together.*

If you make the suede scarf (see Color Plate 11), the ends can be cut long enough to tie, or can be slipped into a scarf clip. I prefer another option, described in the following directions.

Supplies needed:
Fabric: 1/2 yd. (46cm) Facile or Ultrasuede; 1/2 yd. (46cm) scrap fabric
Miscellaneous: leather punches (I used the type that are screwed into a tube handle; see Sources of Supplies); heavy cardboard pieces; small scissors for cutting leather; rotary cutter and mat

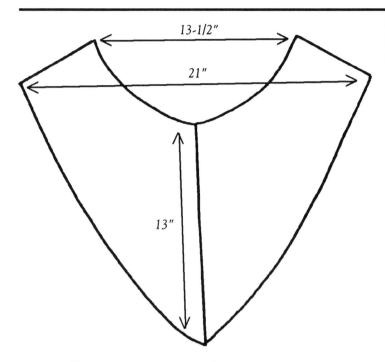

4.41 *Neckline insert from a commercial pattern*

4.42 *Add long pointed end to one side and slightly elongate the other side; then fold over short side and stitch into a channel.*

Soft suedes such as Facile work beautifully for a scarf. Ultrasuede can also be used, but it is stiffer and doesn't drape as well. The pattern I used came from a commercial dress pattern with a kerchieflike insert at the center front.

Before cutting the pattern out of suede, cut it from a piece of old cotton fabric, adding to the length of both ends as shown. One end is still shorter than the other; fold that end under and stitch it into a loop. Slip the other, longer end through it to wear.

Once you're pleased with the cotton pattern,

cut it out of suede using a rotary cutter and mat so the edges are clean.

Use a water-erasable pen (a vanishing marker is fine, too), a plastic circle stencil, and a clear 12" (30.5cm) ruler to measure between the holes.

Then start at the point of the kerchief and draw a circle. From there,

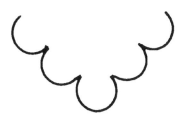

4.43 *Start making scallops from center front.*

travel along each side, drawing scallops with 1/2" (13mm) diameters that touch. Do the same at the neck edge of the kerchief. Then measure up from the edge through the center of each scallop and draw a line at least 2" (5cm) long. On that line make an intersecting mark at a point 1/2" (13mm) from the scalloped edge. Begin punch-

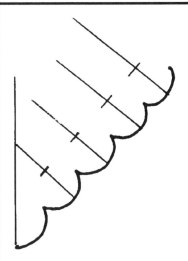

4.44 *In center of scallops, draw lines up from edge and cross them with intersecting lines as a guide for punching holes.*

ing holes, starting at the intersecting line. I used several punch sizes on the long line, but to prevent confusion, I tried to follow my own rule of always finishing one punch size or one line of punches before going on to the next. Because the

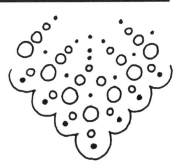

4.45 *Hole design used on the scarf*

suede is thin, you must place several layers of cardboard under it before you tap out the holes.

Once the borders are marked (there's no need to mark every hole as you can eyeball them quite easily), cut out the scallops with small scissors. For precision, first cut one-half curve on each scallop all the

4.46 *Guide for the top edge*

way around. Then flip the scarf and finish cutting the other side of each scallop.

To finish the scarf, you can continue with my design or create one of your own.

To make my design, draw a line down the center of the scarf and evenly space three dots on it (these are where you'll place the motifs I used).

4.47 *Draw line down the center and mark.*

Punch out one of the motifs from scrap suede to use as a pattern. Hold it on top over the measuring marks you've drawn, and draw a dot at every point where you want a hole punched. Making this sample pattern keeps mistakes at a minimum. By using the

4.48 *Punch holes in sample suede to use as a guide.*

pattern over the marks, you can see exactly where you'll place each pattern, each motif is exactly the same, and you can keep the pattern from running into some other part of your design.

After finishing the center, measure and punch out only one side of the vertical mark so you can keep the sides symmetrical. When one side is completed, fold the scarf in the middle and mark through the holes to the unpunched side.

Go back and punch tiny holes at a point 2" (5cm) or halfway between design elements. Punch small holes at the edge of the pointed end, too, and add one of the flower motifs in the center.

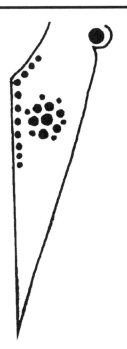

4.49 *Pattern for pointed end*

Wash out the marker ink and dry the scarf flat on a towel.

To wear the scarf, wrap it around your neck, slip the pointed end through the channel at the other side, pull up on the end until it's adjusted to where you want to wear it, then scrunch it down casually in front. It looks sensational over a sweater or a denim shirt, and it's dressy enough to wear with a suit.

4.50 *Paint Indian symbols on suede.*

Afterthought: Use Southwestern designs. Cut out more scarves and use fabric paint to decorate them with Indian symbols, then bead or fringe them.

Don't limit yourself to chamois colors; visit fabric stores to see the range of beautiful suede colors available. Instead of scarves, make collars to attach to jackets or blouses. Make removable collars, too. You may prefer a lacier edge than mine and punch the border wider than I did, or you may want instead to use only small holes, deeper scallops on the edge, or cut points.

Experiment with a scrap of suede and don't limit yourself to round holes only. Use a stencil knife to cut out other geometric or free-form shapes. Look through stencil and cut-work books to find more ideas for the cut-out look. For example, I have a paisley scarf in progress.

If you want to become more familiar with what findings and clasps are available, send for one of the jewelry catalogs in Sources of Supplies.

Now that you know how to make beads, cords, and clasps, you can use this knowledge many ways in the next two chapters.

5. Soft Surfaces

The jewelry I make isn't always covered with beads, doesn't always have a magnificent clasp to recommend it, sometimes has no cord, or sometimes it doesn't have a cord that I haven't used before. It's still jewelry I love. The soft surface projects in this chapter are looped, fringed, feathered, stuffed, and quilted. This is a chapter of ideas illustrating different ways of using the methods already described.

Starting from (soft) scratch

Project 19: Fluffy boa wrap

5.1 *Use the boa as a decorative collar.*

The first project is a boa made of cords, threads, fabric strips, ribbons, and rick-rack (see Color Plates 2 and 13). The 24" (61cm) boas are smashing over plain, long sweaters or knit party dresses. The idea was born when I wrote *Twenty Easy Machine-Made Rugs* (Chilton, 1990). Using a fringe fork is a well-known method of sewing up fluffy rugs, but I decided to make forks of all widths to create textures for clothing, which was challenging and fun.

From my husband's workbench I got the tools I needed. I found a super-big clothes hanger and made a fork 6" (15cm) wide for the boas. Then Bonnie Benson of Quilters' Resources (see Sources of Supplies) sent me a gizmo called "Quick Crafter," which I can adjust for different widths of fringe. I decided to try that, too.

I like using taffeta and silk-types of fabrics along with different widths of taffeta, grosgrain, and satin ribbons. I combined them with furry yarns, cords, rick-rack, and threads. I pulled out combinations from boxes and drawers so I could make choices.

Supplies needed:

Fabric: taffeta, silkies cut in strips

Ribbons, yarn, braid: satin, taffeta, grosgrain ribbon, soutache, rick-rack, furry yarns, assorted cords

Thread: polyester sewing thread to match couched ribbon or soutache

Miscellaneous: adding machine tape, rotary cutter and mat, 6" x 24" (15cm x 61cm) clear plastic ruler

Once my choices were made, I cut all the fabric on the bias into 1/2"-wide (12mm-wide) strips using the rotary cutter and mat. Length doesn't matter as floating ends add to the interesting texture.

Next, I cut a strip of adding machine tape about 2" (5cm) longer than the boa (it's easier to start within the tape rather than exactly at the end). All the fringe is stitched to the tape to prevent the fringe from twisting before you want it to (a helpful hint from Robbie Fanning).

5.2 *Wrap fringe fork with cords, threads, fabric strips, ribbons and rick-rack.*

If you make your fringe fork, wrap it from back to front with fabric, ribbon, cord, and yarn—holding four or five of these together as you wrap—and stitch down the center using stitch width 3, and stitch length 1.5. I had only a few feet of

one cord, a few more of another, and perhaps yards of another, so I used several cords in several sections and others throughout the whole boa. My primary concern was that it look balanced and even.

As I stitched, I kept wrapping and pushing the stitched fringe to the back of the fork (the fringe feeds off the back). If you use Bonnie's fork, you must remove the bar as you progress and replace it as you continue stitching. I found it no problem, and the strength of her "fork" made this extra step worthwhile, but experiment to find out which implement you prefer.

Then put the fork away. Go back to the beginning of the boa. Zigzag down the center again, only this time stitch over a piece of soutache braid or narrow ribbon, leaving 12" (30.5cm) at the begin-

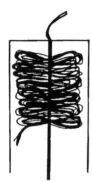

5.3 Zigzag stitch over narrow ribbon.

ning and the end to tie into a bow.

Take the boa off the machine and pull off the adding machine tape. It's been stitched through so many times that it drops off easily. If small pieces of unsightly paper remain, get a permanent marker, a color that blends with the fringes, and color the tape.

Place the ruff around your neck and tie the ribbon into a bow (this looks like part of the fringes). Try twisting the boa before you tie it around your neck—you may like that look, too.

Wear the small boa (see Color Plate 2 and 13) as a decorative collar; stitch up a longer one for a Mae West impersonation.

Project 20: Texas mink

Here's another fluffy necklace you'll enjoy making and wearing (see Color Plate 16). I first saw Texas mink worn by Linda McGhee Williams from Shreveport, LA, who showed me how to make it.

5.4 Texas mink

Supplies needed:
Fabric: one 100 percent cotton bandana (large size if available)
Thread: polyester sewing thread to match
Miscellaneous: rotary cutter and mat, iron, ironing board or pad, 6" x 24" (15cm x 61cm) clear plastic ruler, wash-out marker

All of the construction, except sewing it together, is done on the ironing board. Begin by pressing the bandana,

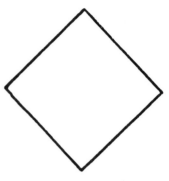

5.5 Press bandana.

then fold it into a triangle and press again.

5.6 Fold into a triangle.

Open it up and use the fold line as a guide.

Pick up opposite corners of the bandana (not the corners bisected by the fold) and place them, touching, on the fold line. Press again and repeat pressing each time you create a fold.

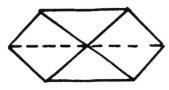

5.7 Open, then bring corners to center.

Fold again by picking up at the outer folds and drawing these to the center. Then fold one

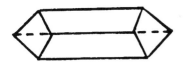

5.8 Bring folded edges to center.

side over the other (the original fold line is now on the outside).

5.9 Fold at center.

Using a ruler and marker, find the midpoint of the folded bandana and draw a line

across the long way. This is the stitching line.

Beginning 6" (15mm) from the point at one end, straight stitch down the length, leaving 6" (15mm) unstitched at the other end (the unstitched ends are the ties). Zigzag

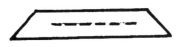

5.10 Straight stitch down center.

over the straight stitch line (stitch width 1.5, stitch length 1.5).

5.11 Zigzag over straight stitches.

Start cutting fringe at a point 6" (15mm) from the bandana point (where the line of stitching starts). To do this easily, place the ruler 1/4" (6mm) over the center stitching line. Using the ruler increments as guides, cut from the fold up to the ruler with a rotary cutter. The ruler keeps the cutter from slicing through the stitching and shows you where to cut so the loops are consistently 1/4" (6mm) wide.

Follow the same procedure on the other side, then cut through the folds to make a fringe. You could also put

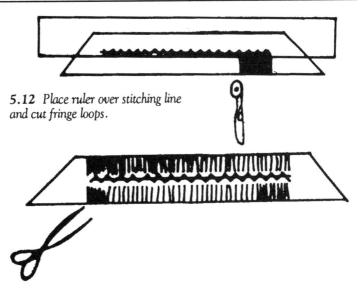

5.12 Place ruler over stitching line and cut fringe loops.

5.13 Go back and cut through folds.

a ruler over the edge and slice off the fold with your rotary cutter.

Thoroughly soak the scarf in water, press out the excess water with your hands, and spin-dry in the dryer. The fringe will fluff up to make Texas mink.

To make longer scarves, use cotton fabrics of your choice and proceed as you did with the bandana square. If you want to make a traditional tie closure, hem the corners first before you begin construction. (For serger owners, use the rolled hem on your machine.) Or, leave the ends unfinished to match the shaggy appearance of your mink.

Project 21: Feather ornaments

Wear both of these feather ornaments on a hat, or use the circular feathers as a lapel pin (see Color Plate 5).

Supplies needed:
Fabric: leather, Ultrasuede, or felt circles 2" (5.1cm) in diameter (leather circles are available at craft and leather stores or cut out your own) for pin; scrap for hat ornament
Feathers: assorted pheasant feathers are ideal as there is a range of color and design, depending upon what part of the pheasant they're found
Thread: monofilament thread, 6" (15cm) tiger tail
Glue: Goop
Needle: hand-sewing
Miscellaneous: shank-type button for lapel pin, pin for attaching to garment or hat, 6" (15cm) tiger tail, beads for stringing, and deer dew claw (optional) for hat ornament

My father hunted pheasants every fall, so I own a pillow case full of pheasant feathers. After cleaning the birds, my mother and I saved the feathers as "possibilities" because they were always too beautiful to throw away. You can buy pheasant feathers and other varieties in all colors, shapes, and sizes at craft, variety, bead, and fabric stores.

These feather ornaments are simple to make—thanks to Goop adhesive—but I prepared all the feathers first before gluing any of them down because working with Goop and feathers is a messy job. To do this, I stripped three 3"-long (7.5cm-long) feathers from midpoint down to the end and cut off the end of a longer feather to make one 6"-long (15cm-long) feather. I also stripped off the fuzzy down found at the bottom of most short feathers.

Feather lapel pin

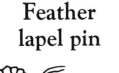

5.14 *Feathered lapel ornament*

For the pin, which is appropriate for a hat, too, I used a leather disk I bought in a package of six at a craft store. I cut to the center from the edge,

5.15 *Cut circle to center, and clip hole there.*

then cut out a tiny hole in the center. Overlapping the cut edges, I glued them together so the disk took on a shallow cone shape. The

5.16 *Overlap edges to create shallow cone.*

point of the cone will be against your body. I spread Goop around the inside of the cone and glued down the row of feathers that would extend slightly beyond the outer edge. Each

5.17 *Overlap and glue feathers to outside edge of cone.*

feather slightly overlaps the one next to it. After that, I glued the bottom of the feathers already in place, then placed another row of the same feathers, cut shorter, so the edges of the first row were still evident. The last row is made up of five shortened feathers of a different design.

5.18 *Glue two more rounds of feathers to cone.*

The three 3"-long (7.5cm-long) feathers are glued to the backing as shown, and a longer 6" (15cm) tail feather extends beyond that.

In the center I used a turquoise and silver earring I'd saved for years (hoping the one I lost would show up). I cut the finding off the back of it and glued it with Goop to the center of my feather motif. A silver button or large turquoise bead in the center can be used.

A pin is attached to the back with several stitches through the leather and the holes in the pin. Slip glue under the ends of the pin as well.

Feather hat ornament

5.19 *Feathered hat ornament*

I began with a pie-shaped piece of Ultrasuede (felt will work, too), which I covered with Goop. I tried to keep the natural arrangement of the wing

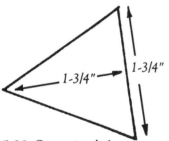

5.20 *Cut a triangle from Ultrasuede.*

feathers intact on this shape. As I pulled a row from the wing feathers, I glued them to the Ultrasuede immediately

and fanned them out (at the wide side opposite the point). Then I pulled off another row, and another, until I ended with a fourth row of short blue/brown wing feathers near the point.

5.21 *Fan out four rows of wing feathers and glue down.*

On the underside of the Ultrasuede (and extending beyond the first fan of feathers I glued down) I glued on six longer feathers, and one long tail feather curves from the middle beyond that group of six.

5.22 *Glue six longer feathers and one long tail feather behind the Ultrasuede.*

On the front point I used a fuzzy feather from a feather duster. I cut it down and glued it on so the feather would cover the quill ends. The Ultrasuede point fit into a deer dew claw (see Sources of Supplies) I had left over from the

5.23 *Add fuzzy feather at point and slip into a deer dew claw or wrap the point and glue down beads.*

Indian medicine necklace (Chapter 6), but you can also create a cone shape from Ultrasuede or Sculpey, or wrap with beads.

Next, I strung 12 pieces of turquoise and three coral pieces onto a piece of tiger tail (plastic over wire), because its

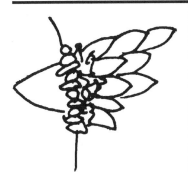

5.24 *String beads on to tiger tail.*

stiffness makes it easier to manage. The beaded tiger tail was stretched around the top of the deer claw, and a square knot was tied at the back. Then I

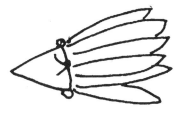

5.25 *Tie a square knot in back.*

slipped Goop under the beads in front and in back to hold them in place.

Once that was finished, I glued a pin to the back of the Ultrasuede with Goop.

Instant Ideas

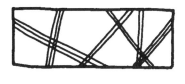

1. *Use a double or triple needle to stitch up fabric. Use curves and sometimes cross stitching. Then cut out the interesting areas for buttons or barrettes.*

2. *Sew down ribbons, and use decorative machine stitches, too, to decorate fabric for barrettes or pins.*

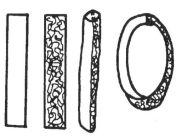

3. *Make a moebius neck piece. Cut out two pieces of fabric the same size (dimensions will depend on the look you want and the fabric itself). Embroider one of the pieces. Make a tube of the two pieces, twist, and overlap to join into a moebius strip.*

Project 22: Fishing fly earrings

5.26 *Fishing fly*

More feathers! But this time we're talking instant earrings (see Color Plates 5 and 7).

The man at the bait shop wasn't surprised when I requested directions to the fishing flies. He showed me a counter of fuzzy, furry, feathery fishing flies as well as a wall of glow-in-the-dark neon beads and other appropriate goodies. "These are popular for jewelry," he said matter-of-factly and pointed out brass barrel-shaped sinkers and a bag of feathers. I got to work evaluating every fishing fly and lure in his establishment.

Feathers, threads, yarn, and beads of every color combine to fool the fish—or decorate your ears. They mimic flies, bumble bees, and insects (but I drew the line at the deer hair mouse). I made my choices, and bought shiny brass and silver spinners, swivels, and snaps, as well as beads to decorate doll pins.

Supplies needed:
Fishing flies: two matching fishing flies
Thread: sewing thread to match flies
Needle: hand-sewing
Miscellaneous: french ear hook, wire cutter

When I got home, I made instant fishing fly earrings by cutting off the hooks of each with a wire cutter, then slipping jump rings in the top loops and attaching french hook earring findings.

5.27 *Hook removed and earring made*

Project 23: Southwestern pins

Making pins is as easy as covering an interesting cardboard shape or decorating a button. I used Southwestern colors,

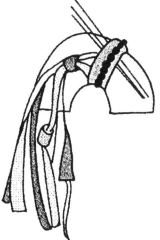

5.28 *Suede covered cardboard decorated with beads, leather strips, feathers, and quills.*

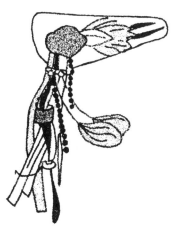

5.29 *Another cardboard shape covered with suede and decorated*

because we can't seem to get enough of them, but you use the colors, beads, and bangles you prefer. The directions remain the same, but you can substitute the ingredients (see Color Plate 9).

To make the pins found on the color pages, gather up the following:

Fabric: Ultrasuede scraps and narrow strips (I cut my own using a ruler and rotary cutter and mat.)
Beads: turquoise, small beads in assorted colors
Glue: Goop
Tools: rotary cutter and mat, scissors for cutting suede, hemostat or needle-nosed pliers
Miscellaneous: natural and dyed porcupine quills, copper metal flash or small flat stones; antler buttons; cardboard for backing

If you don't have these supplies (I'd be surprised if you did), you can get them at many bead shops and craft stores, or through mail order (see Sources of Supplies).

Cut pin shapes out of stiff cardboard and spread Goop over one side. Apply it to the back of a piece of Ultrasuede that is slightly larger than the cardboard. Cut the Ultrasuede back to 1/4"

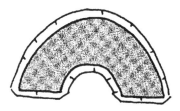

5.30 *Cut out a cardboard pattern and glue to suede. Clip in suede edges and clip off corners.*

(6mm) around the edge of the cardboard. Clip suede up to the cardboard all around the edge and cut bulk from the corners. Then spread Goop along the back edge of the cardboard and pull the suede around the cardboard to the back. A hemostat or pliers helps

5.31 *Bring suede to back and glue in place.*

here to pull the suede tightly—but not so tight that the pin bows. Decorate the pin with beads, quills, and strips of suede. Check the color pages or use your own imagination.

Spread Goop lightly across the back of the cardboard, then place it on another piece of Ultrasuede (attach a safety pin or commercial pin to this backing first).

5.32 *Apply backing and pin.*

After the backing is applied cut around it, slightly inside the edge of the pin.

These simple pins can be used on a chamois tube necklace (see Color Plate 9) or as earrings, too. The following antler pin project is another Southwestern (or northern Wisconsin) idea.

Instant Ideas

4. *Roll edges of two pieces of organdy or reversible fabric with a serger, or use a fine satin stitch on your sewing machine (Optional: Use a scallop stitch at the edges.) Stack the two pieces of fabric, then stitch them together down the center with a double needle—channel must have room enough for a ribbon. Slip ribbon through center and draw up into ruff to wear as collar.*

5. *Embroider or paint a necklace on a tee shirt or sweatshirt. Glue on gems, add studs and shisha mirrors (tiny mirrors approximately 1" [2.5cm] in diameter—or use paillettes). Stitch on tassels. Use your imagination.*

Project 24: Antler button pin

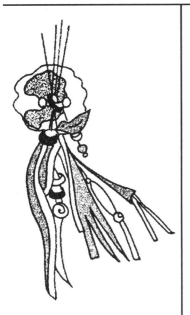

5.33 *Large antler button decorated and made into a pin*

Supplies needed:

Base: deer antler button, wooden, or large clay two-hole button (1-1/2" x 1" [4cm x 2.5cm])

Fabric: 4 colors of Ultrasuede cut into strips approximately 6" x 1/4" (15cm x 6mm) long

Beads: 6 small turquoise beads, assorted brass beads, 1 pony bead

Glue: Goop

Miscellaneous: 3 porcupine quills, 1 piece of flattened, free-form copper flash or small flat stone, 1 copper eye pin, 1 small pearl bird

Glue a piece of copper flash (use Goop) between the two holes of the button, or substitute a flat bead or turquoise chunk (see Color Plate 9).

Pull three suede strips through the holes to the back of the button as shown. String turquoise beads on double polyester thread or bead stringing

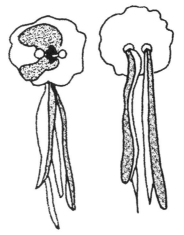

5.34 *To decorate the button glue copper flash (or flat stone) between holes. Then thread laces through holes. String up beads and tie them around center strips, holding them in place with a square knot.*

thread. Sew around the center strips and tie into a square knot. Dot the knot with glue.

Slip porcupine quills between copper and suede strips. Attach eye pin with beads and small pearl bird to the same center strips.

With fourth suede strip, tie off the three others and pull both ends through a pony bead.

5.35 *Pull laces through a pony bead and continue to decorate.*

Decorate strips with the assortment of beads, tie knots at end of strips, or glue invisibly inside the bead. Cut strips into different lengths.

Project 25: Doll pins

5.36 *Doll pin ideas*

Here are general directions for the next pin idea (see Color Plates 2, 3, and 9) which can look like the Southwest or Mars or anywhere in between. I designed a tiny doll pattern to use as the basic design for any wild or conservative lapel pin I can dream up. The arms are perfect hangers for every odd bangle, bead, bell, or junk I can find. I use eye or head pins to string on tiny beads or fetishes. Sometimes I use fishing swivels at the hands so I can tie feathers or strips of suede to them, or I string beads from one hand to the other.

I usually sew a button over the blank face, then decorate between the holes with strings of beads.

On top and in back of the head I sew down feathers, yarn, rick-rack, beads—it's an important area and, along with the button face, determines the personality of the doll.

The same doll pattern is used for all the pins (see color pages), but they all look different depending on the fabric used, or how they're decorated.

First, make two patterns out of heavy see-through plastic. The first pattern includes a 1/8" (3mm) seam allowance; for the second pattern, leave off the 1/8" (3mm) seam allowance. Place the smaller pattern on the wrong side of your fabric and draw around it. Go back with the larger pattern, place it over the drawing, and draw around that, too. (Don't cut out the doll yet.)

Hint: If you need only one copy of a design, use a copy machine. One transfer per copy is possible. First, run off the copy, then turn it design-side down on fabric and press with a hot iron.

Pin the pattern right sides together with another piece of fabric. Straight stitch (stitch length 1.5) around the inside stitching line of the doll. Now cut out the doll on the outside stitching line and use zigzag stitch (stitch width

5.38 *Stitch around doll, then clip down the back for stuffing.*

1.5, stitch length 1) on the seam allowance.

Then clip down the back about 1" (2.5cm) for turning right side out later. Clip in at corners and curves, then use a hemostat to turn the fabric by inserting the tool down into the ends of the arms and legs, grasping the fabric, and pulling the doll right side out.

Stuff the doll with fiberfill. Push the filling in tightly with a dull-pointed instrument (I use the handle of a crochet hook). Stitch the opening closed.

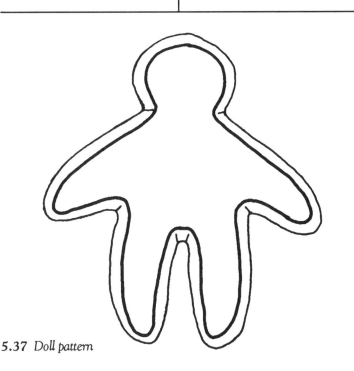

5.37 *Doll pattern*

Indian doll pin

For the Indian doll you'll need Ultrasuede, suede, or chamois scraps for the body (see Color Plates 9 and 11). Use button faces—I use antler buttons when I have them, and sometimes I use slices of birch tree limbs or clay buttons (don't forget Sculpey or cornstarch buttons).

Supplies needed:

Fabric: Ultrasuede, suede, or chamois scraps

Thread: polyester sewing in suede colors or monofilament

Needle: hand-sewing

Glue: Goop

Embellishments: assorted small seed beads, buttons, bangles, charms, bells and bead caps, swivels, cones, washers, sequins, porcupine quills, feathers, fur scraps, twigs (the choice is yours)

Miscellaneous: antler buttons, wooden or clay two-hole buttons for face, fiberfill, scissors for cutting suede, pin finding

I beaded, fringed, and tied up the dolls with suede strips. Gather up all the junky earrings, beads, findings, washers, sequins, feathers, and quills you can find. I used small pieces of fur, also.

Most of the decoration was sewn on, but at times I found that glue is better, and Goop is perfect because it doesn't soak into the fabric or suede.

Each doll is different, which also makes it special.

Hint: When I used the pattern for Indian dolls, I made some of them in two parts (the top part was longer than a pattern

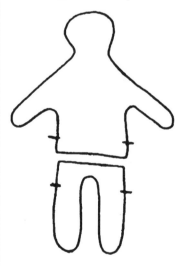

5.39 *Make a two-part pattern using a long top.*

half to allow for the join). Then I could construct the leggings by stitching right sides together on the inside of

5.40 *Sew and clip fringe.*

the legs, turning, then stuffing, and finishing the stitching down at the sides of the legs from the right side. After sewing the legs and stuffing them, I clipped the fringe at the sides of the legs. Only then did I sew the two parts together by overlapping the legs with the top part and stitching

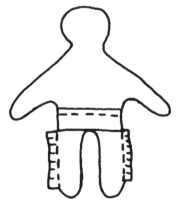

5.41 *Stitch top and bottom together.*

them together on the sewing machine. If you want to hide the stitching line, tie a suede belt around it or glue on a wider piece of suede fringed at the bottom.

Another method I use is cutting a pattern with enough fabric at the underarms for fringe. Stitch right sides together, leaving the seams open at the underarms. After turning and stuffing, I stitch the arms together above the fringe and clip the fringe to the stitching line.

5.42 *Clip fringe under arm.*

Doll pins with glitz

Choose a glitzy fabric, such as a polyester knit with a gold or silver surface. I sometimes patch different fabrics together first, then draw my doll pattern across the patches to include several patterns. The clear plastic allows you to place the pattern exactly where you want it on the patches. Proceed marking, sewing, and cutting out the doll as in the previous general doll directions.

5.43 *Other doll ideas*

Once the doll is sewn together and stuffed with fiberfill, the fun begins. Add beads, feathers, buttons, twigs, charms, yarn, rick-rack, sequins, fishing swivels, bells, bead caps, or anything you have in your junk drawer to embellish it. Cover the stitched opening with a pin, stitching it in place.

Make denim dolls and add metal jeans buttons and shredded bandana hair; make a quilt or sewing doll decorated with snaps, needles, pins, a thimble for the head, with a hole at the top to add strings of beads, grommets, and other notions; or make lace dolls and add silk ribbons, flowers, crystal beads, and pearl buttons. You'll never be able to stop at making just one doll pin; and my only fear is that you may live near my favorite thrift shop (my jewelry junk finds there are sometimes hilarious but always worth the trip to make my doll pins not-of-this-world).

Project 26: Muslin and paint pins

5.44 Muslin designs

5.45 *Otto design with quilting lines*

We've all seen china plates made with children's original drawings fired onto them or drawings turned into appliqués, which mothers sew onto pillows. I had the idea of painting on muslin to make pins (see Color Plate 15) when I looked through my collection of drawings our granddaughters have given me over the years (I knew there was a reason for not throwing away any of them).

I especially wanted to make the dog pin because it is a likeness of our deceased wire-haired

dachshund, Otto. (I liken Otto to Elvis. Both are long gone, but no one will let them be.) A tiny Otto appears, like a signature, on every school paper our son Steve, and now grand-daughter Julie, has handed in.

Jennifer's drawing of a clown is from kindergarten, though she can't remember and she won't

5.46 *Jennifer's clown*

take responsibility for it. I dug out the most simple, naive drawings, which is what I needed for these pins. If a drawing is too complicated, I simplify it.

Supplies needed:
Fabric: plain muslin
Thread: matching thread, monofilament
Paint: acrylics in assorted colors or fabric paints, fine black permanent markers (other colors optional)
Miscellaneous: transfer pencil (optional), iron and cloth for pressing, scissors, fiberfill, beads and baubles, pin back, newspapers, paint brushes

My copy machine is a big help when I need to enlarge or reduce the original designs. Once I print one that's a good pin size, I hold it up to the window under the muslin so I can draw the design on the fabric with a water-soluble marker, or I trace around the design with a transfer pencil, then iron the pattern onto the muslin.

The designs I used here are from the children's drawings, or adapted from Dahomey African appliqués, because I like them so much; several are drawings from my own notebooks.

Before you begin dye-painting the designs, draw the design outlines on the muslin with a fine, black, permanent marker.

Instead of coloring the designs with thick paint, I used watered-down acrylic paints to dye the fabric. I started with a ratio of three parts water to one part paint, which I mixed up in a saucer. I was never exact and usually I liked the results when I used more water. However, sometimes I wanted certain areas more colorful. Oh my, you can see that I ended up with many, many saucers! You'll understand what I mean about not being exact when you

experiment on scrap fabric with the ratio of water to paint. Do this by dunking a paint brush in the watery paint, removing the excess by brushing over newspaper, then painting the muslin with the damp brush. Try adding more colors, painting with a wetter brush and letting colors run and blend into other colors. It's not exact, it's a lot of fun, and I think you'll like the effect better than if you use heavy paint. Yes, you can use undiluted acrylics if you wish, or fabric crayons. Try them all; then decide.

If you want to add highlights of dots or heavy lines, wait until the fabric is dry or almost dry and add undiluted paint dots and lines. (You can speed drying by using a hair dryer.)

When the painting is completed and dry, press it (cover first with a press cloth) with an iron. Then place the front of the design down on the right side of another piece of fabric (don't cut out the design or backing yet).

Straight stitch around at stitch length 1.5 setting (you can see the outline through the fabric). Cut out the design 1/8" (3mm) from the stitching line. Clip in the corners and cut off points and excess seam allowance. Go back and stitch around with stitch width 1.5 and stitch length 1.

Slit down the backing (the pin will hide the stitching) and turn the shape to the right side. Stuff the pin lightly and stitch up the opening by hand with a whip stitch.

Machine quilt from the top with monofilament if you wish. Remember that too much stitching flattens the pins. Add beads and baubles, too, by hand or machine. Then sew a safety pin or commercial pin to the back.

As a den mother, a room mother, as well as a Girl Scout helper-outer, I was always trying to come up with something original for gifts for mothers; the pin project is for all of you who still hold those jobs. The scouts can draw and color the pictures at one meeting. Transfer the design to fabric using a transfer pencil; then let the scouts color them with fabric crayons.

If the kids need design ideas, find *Ed Emberley's Drawing Book of Animals* (Little Brown, 1970). He shows how to draw simple bugs and animals by a progression of simple lines, which can be used for designs for muslin pins.

Once the designs are drawn, sew up the pins, cut them out, and let the children fill them with batting. They can sew up the opening at the back (teach them how). You do the quilting, but the children can sew on beads—and that means the boys, too.

Attach a pin.

Afterthought: To make a pin more quickly, find printed fabric with animals, fish, or people on it. Cut out the designs, back with other fabric, then stitch, stuff, and use those for pins.

Project 27:
Button covers and earrings

5.47 *Make a button cover.*

The findings needed for button covers are available now at craft stores. They either are hinged or can slide in place over a plain button. Don't forget to use them on the cuffs of long-sleeved blouses to imitate cuff links (see Color Plate 7).

Supplies needed:
Fabric: 12" x 12" (31cm x 31cm)
Cord: 2 yds. (1.8m) copper-colored cord
Glue: Goop
Miscellaneous: button backings

First find a fabric you love (I chose a dark, jewel-tone print), then a cord or heavy thread (mine is heavy copper thread) that looks terrific

with it, Magic Tape, glue stick, Goop, and the button covers and earring backs (we'll make earrings to match the buttons).

Cut fabric on the bias (12" x 1-1/2" [31cm x

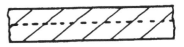

5.48 *Cut strips on the bias.*

4cm]). Run glue stick across back, then fold both long sides to the

5.49 *Fold long sides to meet in the center.*

center. Glue again and fold down the center.

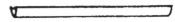

5.50 *Fold down center.*

Cut lengths of copper thread the same length as the fabric. Tape copper to one end of fabric. Twist the bias strip into a narrow cord, then hold one end of the copper thread and fabric cord

5.51 Twist the fabric, then tape cord to fabric and twist again.

together in one hand. In the other hand, hold the other ends together, too. Twist these two until so tight they twist back on themselves (like monks' cord; see Chapter 3). Fold under one end and spiral around the center and out to the edge of the cover. Then, to keep the

5.52 Spiral from center out.

circle from unrolling, poke a threaded needle from the top, down, and from one side to another.

5.53 Stitch from top down, and side to side to hold spiral in place.

Tuck the end underneath and glue to secure. Clip off the end if it's too long and bulky.

5.54 Clip off extra fabric, then slip end under and glue.

Cover the top of the button cover with Goop. Press the button top onto the Goop and hold it in place a few seconds.

Use Goop to glue the fabric circles to button covers or earring backings. Make button covers from Sculpey, too, and don't limit the following rick-rack flowers to earrings only—make button covers.

Afterthought: Fabric can be dipped into Stiffy or a mixture of three parts water, one part white glue. I don't do this because I want to retain the softness of the fabric.

Instant Idea

6. *Cover cardboard shape with batting and silk. String a few beads on to gold or silver cord and wrap around the cardboard several times. Slip the beads along the cord until the placement pleases you, then glue the cord in place in back. Stitch pin backing to suede and glue suede to the back of the pin.*

Project 28: Rick-rack earrings

5.55 *Rick-rack flower earrings*

These flower earrings are soft, too (see Color Plate 10). Made of rick-rack, they match the necklace in Chapter 3.

Supplies needed:
Rick-rack: 2 yds. (1.8m)
Thread: polyester sewing thread matching rick-rack
Needle: hand-sewing
Glue: Goop
Miscellaneous: earring post or clip findings, vanishing marker, ruler

You need 2 yards (1.8m) of rick-rack for one pair of earrings. Cut it into 1 yard (.9m) pieces. Then fold the rick-rack pieces in half and interlock by hooking each together.

Fold in half again and make a mark with a vanishing marker or pin.

5.56 *Fold rick-rack in half and interlock.*

Next, hide the raw end by folding it down, then roll the strip back on itself up to the mark to create a bud. With a hand-sewing needle and doubled thread, stitch the under points to hold the bud together. Leave the

5.57 *Wind, hold bottom points together, and stitch.*

needle and thread dangling while you finish the flower.

5.58 *At the end of the rick-rack, fold under the raw edge and tack.*

Continue by wrapping and folding down the outer points to create petals. Circle the bud twice with petals, and at the same time finger press the top points down. Use the needle and thread to poke in and out through the bottom points to hold the flower together. Pull up tightly as you stitch. At the end, fold back the raw edge and tack to underside.

Use a large drop of Goop on an earring base and press the flower into it to make a lovely flower earring.

Depending on the rick rack width, the flower is appropriate for lapel pins, shoe clips, or barrettes.

Rick-rack pin or shoe clip

To make the large flower (see Color Plate 10), I found jumbo rick-rack at a fabric outlet store (the same rick-rack as I've seen on designer dresses recently). Although I created the large flower the same as I did the earrings, I experimented with size. The size is contingent on the width of the rick-rack, but also on the effect I wanted. I can make several of these for a barrette or hair ornament, or make a pair for shoe clips. For this one, I sewed a pin backing to the flower to wear on a lapel.

Recycling scraps and samples

Do you have a box of embroidered scraps and samples that you'll never finish (you aren't even interested in finishing), yet you can't throw away? I do. Some of my experiments were never completed because they ended up less than perfect (like, a mess), were only for play, I lacked the time, I didn't like the colors, or a birthday had passed. Sometimes after I learned how to do certain stitches or techniques, I wasn't interested in doing any more. My problem is that I can't part with any of these incomplete projects. They overflow a box in a cupboard where I can discover them periodically. I look through them with the thought that some day I'll find a use for them. The day came when I decided to recycle them into pins, and chose the ever-popular heart shape for starters (see Color Plates 3, 12, and 13).

Instant Idea

7. *Paint, then stitch up tiny muslin fish. Fill (use thin layer) by slipping in batting the same size as the fish. Hang several from nylon cord and attach them to an earring finding for each ear.*

Project 29: Heart pins and barrettes

5.59 *Heart designs for pins*

Supplies needed:
Fabric: embroidered fabric pieces—discards or old, embroidered scraps of fabrics
Thread: sewing thread to match embroideries, thread for tassels
Miscellaneous: fiberfill, assorted beads, pin and barrette backings, cardboard (optional), scissors, monk's cord (optional)

First I made several sizes of heart templates from see-through plastic so I'd be able to zero in on exactly what part of my embroidery to use (you can buy sets from quilting stores). Once I decided, I used a marker to draw around the heart shape that fit the embroidery best and drew a 1/4" (6.4mm) seam allowance, too.

Now I had several options. Bead first, then cut out and fold under the edges of the beaded top and plain bottom

5.60 Bead pin, then turn under edges, fill with fiberfill.

fabric, stitching the edges together (except for a small area), then filling the heart with fiberfill and sewing it shut. The edges are left as is or covered with beads or cord to hide the stitches.

5.61 Sew shut with ladder stitch.

Alternatively, you could place right sides of the heart together on a backing fabric, stitch

around the design, then cut it out and zigzag around the edge. Slit up

5.62 Stitch and cut out hearts, then zigzag at edge. Clip down center back.

the back of the heart and turn it right side out, filling it, sewing it shut, then beading it. It's not

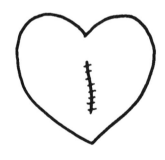

5.63 Turn, fill, and stitch shut.

difficult to do, and sometimes I prefer this method. You could also finish the piece as described in making pendants.

But what if you are among the minority that doesn't save scraps or samples? Then find fabric you can embroider—use a print and embellish the design with embroidery or use beads only. Try covering a flowered or plain fabric with lace and bead that, too.

If your pin is large enough, you can slip monk's cord through the attaching pin and wear it as a pendant.

5.64 Change pin to pendant by threading a cord through the pin.

Making tassels

On many of my re-cycled pins (see Color Plates 3, 12, and 13) I added strings of beads like tassels, or I added tassels. I like to use monk's cord around the edges and tie a bow at the top of the heart and make a tassel at the bottom with the same cord.

5.65 *Cover the edges with cord and make bows at top and bottom with same cord. Finish off with a tassel.*

Tassels are easy to make: first cut a piece of cardboard the length of the tassel. Wrap the cardboard with yarn, cord, or thread until you achieve the desired thickness; then tie a short piece of cord at the top. Clip the yarn from the cardboard at the bottom.

5.66 *Wrap cord around a piece of cardboard. Tie the cords off at the top.*

Place a wrapping cord next to the tassel, loop it at the top, then bring the

5.67 *Lay cord next to threads.*

wrapping cord down to the bottom and wrap from there, up around the tassel, and place the end of the cord through the loop at top. Pull down on

5.68 *Wrap and then slip through loop.*

the other end of the wrapping cord to bring the loop down, inside of wrap. Clip the end. (I refer to this as a tassel wrap.)

5.69 *Pull down so loop is hidden.*

5.70 *Decorate tassel by stitching beads to the top cords.*

5.71 *Cover the top with buttonhole stitches.*

5.72 *Satin stitch over wire and wrap it around the tassel.*

Decorate the tassel with beads or more embroidery. Don't limit yourself to decorating pins; instead, use tassels alone for earrings, or at the ends of necklaces and key chains, or on hats. And use satin stitches over wire instead of a wrapping cord to wrap the tassel. For another look, you may want to slip a tiny cork bead in the top to fill out the area before wrapping.

I also make barrettes with recycled embroideries and sewing machine lace. You'll find three of them on the color pages. One is a barrette of a needle-weaving experiment where the warp and weft threads of a loosely woven fabric were drawn out; I then used the sewing machine to zigzag

other threads together into a lacy, see-through fabric. I backed this with another color, then made a colorful barrette from the results.

The white lace, beaded barrette is a piece of machine-made lace that didn't turn out as I had wanted. I was experimenting with tension settings on the top and bobbin. Instead of throwing it away, I backed it

Plate 13

Clockwise from top left. ■ Fluffy boa, made from fabric, yarn, braid, rick-rack, ribbons. ■ Machine-embroidered heart with beads, tassel, pin back. ■ Wind brocade ribbons around plastic straws, add brass beads; string both on satin ribbon. ■ Pour casting resin over marbleized paper to make earrings. ■ Pillowbead necklace. ■ Barrette made of recycled needlelace.

Plate 14

Top left to lower right. ■ Earrings of Sulky variegated thread stitched on stabilizer. ■ Favorite decorative machine stitches are used to make pillow beads for necklace. ■ Purchased beaded Christmas ornament made into instant pendant. ■ Rayon braid completes hand-embroidered pendant. ■ Another hand-embroidered pendant, suspended on monk's cord. ■ Map of your favorite city or vacation spot, covered with casting resin and glued to earring findings!

Plate 15
Clockwise from top left. ■ Muslin clown, based on child's drawing. ■ Painted, quilted, beaded muslin bird. ■ Fish pin. ■ Another fish, this one with torn strips of fabric for tail. ■ Quilt, then add bells to painted face. ■ Child's drawing of family pet, transferred to muslin. ■ Fish, dangle charm. ■ Quilted and beaded lion. ■ Imaginary animals with polka dots and beads; note that seed bead teeth lend a ferocious look. *Center:* Bias tape tubes make clown's arms and legs.

Plate 16

Clockwise from top center. ■ Photo earrings, coated with casting resin. ■ Denim and rick-rack earrings. ■ Necklace of wrapped and wound denim beads, red flannel spacers. ■ Fabric tube necklace, made by alternating knots and beads. ■ Glue earring backings to ready-made red stars. ■ Fold, sew, and fringe a bandana necklace.

with a piece of fabric, then beaded over my mistakes. No one can tell that the lace is not wonderful looking because most of it is hidden with beads.

The third barrette is the easiest. I had strips of embroidered fabric left from my first pillow bead experiments (see page 22), so I clipped a piece into a barrette form and it looks like I planned it that way. I'm on a recycling roll.

In Chapter 6 we'll continue to make jewelry, but not all of it soft. Instead, we'll spray, dip or paint on coatings to protect and make the soft jewelry more rigid, and cover a soft elastic base with buttons to make a bracelet copy of an antique idea.

Instant Ideas

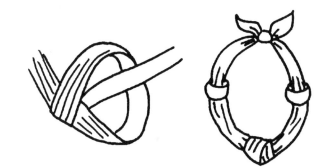

8. *Fold up bandana or scarf as in Texas mink, then tie an overhand knot in center. Add a large macramé bead at each side, if you wish, then tie it at the back for a closure.*

9. *Make a tube of flowered chintz (leaving a few extra inches at each end) to cover foam-covered hair curlers. Insert flowers and ribbons at each end and tie or make a tassel wrap at each end (this looks like a party favor). Wear it around a pony tail.*

Instead of hair curlers, chenille covered wire (available at craft stores) works as a filling for small tubes. Make original pony tail twists or use them for bracelets.

6. Soft Cores and Hard Surfaces

Although you don't expect to find directions for making hard surfaces in a soft jewelry book, most of the following started out soft. If the jewelry is then coated with a laminate, or resin, or stiffened with the residue from water-soluble stabilizer, I've placed it in this chapter.

The Indian medicine necklace is a combination of leather, suede, feathers, furs, bone, and plastic, and this seemed to be the only fitting place for this conglomeration of soft and hard properties.

Also included are button bracelets, made by sewing buttons to waistband elastic. The button earrings include beads and sequins, but also soutache braid—only a hint of softness, but softness nonetheless.

Using water-soluble stabilizer

The first projects in this section, all earrings, are machine stitched on water-soluble stabilizer, a wonderful invention. Water-soluble stabilizer opens up a new world for machine embroiderers. It allows us to stitch as if we were sewing on fabric. After stitching, the stabilizer is dissolved by holding it under a faucet or soaking it in a pan of water so that only the stitched threads remain.

On the following earrings I use it to hold scraps of fabrics together while they're being stitched and attached with metallic thread, and also to hold together stitches when there is no fabric.

Project 30: Lace earrings

6.1 Lace earring pattern

Jan Saunders of Dublin, OH, showed me how to make lace earrings (see Color Plate 10). To do so, I collected the following supplies:

Thread: #8 pearl cotton on bobbin, machine-embroidery thread to match pearl cotton

Miscellaneous: water-soluble stabilizer, small spring hoop, one pair post earrings or ear wires, white opaque marker

For these earrings, place a double layer of water-soluble stabilizer in the hoop and draw a design on the stabilizer using the white opaque marker. Use a continuous line to create a star burst, snowflake, or flower design.

Set machine to free stitching—feed dogs lowered or covered. Begin by dipping the needle down to bring up the bobbin thread. Hold to one side—don't anchor it. You'll sew over the tail and it can be cut off as soon as you do.

Begin to freely stitch in your design on the stabilizer. Continue until you've completed the earring to your satisfaction. Stitch with a continuous line and keep joining and crossing stitches where necessary to make it all hang together when the stabilizer is dissolved.

Then complete the second earring. Don't try to make it exactly the same as the first—it's not important and almost impossible.

Take the stabilizer out of the hoop and cut out around the lace. Dissolve the stabilizer out of the threads by holding the earrings under running water, but leave a bit of goo in the threads to stiffen them after pressing.

Pull the lace carefully into shape and press with an iron between two pieces of fabric. Lift, to loosen from the fabric, and let dry completely (or it may stick to the fabric).

Wear the lace earrings by poking a post earring through one of the petals or hang them from ear wires.

Project 31:
Scraps and lace earrings

6.2 Scrap lace earring pattern

Supplies needed:

Fabric: tiny scraps of many colors

Thread: gold metallic machine-embroidery

Miscellaneous: water-soluble stabilizer, small spring hoop, kidney wire earring findings, white opaque marker, scissors

For these earrings (see Color Plate 8), I cut up pieces of colorful, silky fabrics, arranging them in two small triangles between the two pieces of stabilizer. With gold metallic thread on the top and bobbin, I stitched in a haphazard manner but made sure to sew through all the tiny fabric pieces so they hang together. Then I sewed two small circles (one on top of the other) at the top to hold the earring findings.

After taking the earrings out of the hoop, I dissolved the water-soluble stabilizer and hung them from kidney wires.

Make stained glass earrings (see Color Plate 12) the same way as scraps and lace earrings, except layer scraps of transparent fabrics, completely covering the triangle outline. After freely stitching the scraps together, use a narrow zigzag stitch to create a border around the earrings. Wash out part of the stabilizer, then clip off any fabric past the zigzag stitches to clean up the edges. Pinch the earrings into three-dimensional shapes while still damp.

Thread earrings on water-soluble stabilizer

The next projects also include directions for stitching earrings on water-soluble stabilizer. Metallic threads are used on the first two; the completed earrings are not lacey, but solid threads and braids.

Variegated threads are used for three other earring ideas. With controlled stitching, you can create plaid earrings.

Project 32: Gold triangle earrings

The first earrings are small, beaded triangles created from layers of gold metallic stitches (see Color Plate 12). Metallic thread doesn't pack down as tightly as rayon or cottons, so the earrings are more attractive.

Supplies needed:

Stitch width: 0 to medium
Stitch length: 0
Feed dogs: lowered or covered
Presser foot: darning foot or spring
Needle: #90/14 sharp
Tension: top, loosened; bobbin, normal
Thread: gold metallic machine embroidery
Fabric: 1/4" (6mm) square scraps to match gold thread (cut out 2)
Accessories: permanent white opaque marker, 5" (13cm) or 7" (18 cm) spring hoop, glue stick, epoxy (2 tube type) or Goop
Stabilizer: water-soluble
Miscellaneous: 40 small (2mm) beads to match earrings, earring clips or posts

Place gold metallic thread on the top of the machine and wind a bobbin of the same thread. Cover or lower the feed dogs and set the machine on "0" stitch width and length.

Clip two layers of water-soluble stabilizer into a spring hoop. I use larger spring hoops because then I can make several pairs of earrings at one time.

Draw the outline of your triangles on the stabilizer with the white marker. Slip the hoop

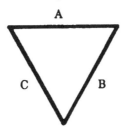

6.3 *Pattern for thread triangle earrings. Draw two outlines on water-soluble stabilizer.*

under the needle; then dip the needle down to bring up the bobbin thread and hold it to one side. Stitch around the outline twice, then clip

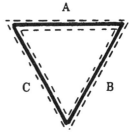

6.4 *Stitch twice around the perimeters of the triangles.*

off the thread tail. Next, fill in the triangle with straight stitches. Keep

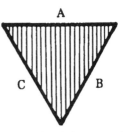

6.5 *Straight stitch in rows down from the top edge of the triangle.*

the rows of stitches close together, but not on top of each other. If the stabilizer tears, slip a small scrap of it under the tear to repair it.

After the triangle is filled in, turn the hoop a quarter turn and straight stitch up and down as you travel across the earring.

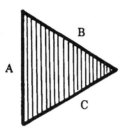

6.6 *Turn the hoop and straight stitch across the triangle, perpendicular to the first pass.*

Before the third pass, place the tiny scrap of matching fabric underneath the earring where you'll glue the clip or post later. (This is Jane Warnick's idea—the fabric prevents the glue from soaking into the layers of stitches.) You may want to place a small dot of glue stick between the scrap of fabric and earring to help hold the fabric in place when you stitch.

On this final pass, change stitch width to medium zigzag before traveling back and forth across the earring. Blend in the stitches evenly to prevent satin stitch

ridges. When you reach edges B and C, go slightly beyond them to create a soft fringe. With your

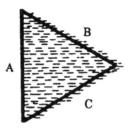

6.7 *Zigzag at a medium width to fill in the triangle and fringe the edge at the same time.*

machine still set on medium stitch width, satin stitch down the edge of side A. Move the

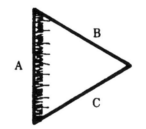

6.8 *Finish edge A with medium satin stitches.*

hoop so the stitches go off the edge on the left swing, but stitch on the earring on the right swing. Every few stitches, stitch sideways into the earring to anchor the ridge securely. Go back and repeat the last row without side stitching to make a smoothly finished edge.

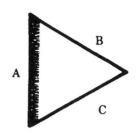

6.9 *Satin stitch over edge again.*

Take the stabilizer out of the hoop and cut around the earrings to remove most of the stabilizer. Hold the earrings under a faucet to wash out the rest of it; then place them between two layers of toweling and squeeze out the moisture. Next, use a hand-sewing needle and a doubled gold thread to stitch the beads in place.

6.10 *Hand sew beads to earrings.*

Mix the epoxy and follow directions on the package to glue the backings to the earrings, or use a drop of Goop instead. Let the glue dry thoroughly before wearing.

Project 33: Gold braid rectangles

The second pair of earrings is made up of gold ribbon thread, or narrow gold braid on the bobbin and gold metallic thread on the top of the machine (see Color Plate 12).

Supplies needed:
Stitch width: 0
Stitch length: 0
Feed dogs: lowered or covered
Presser foot: darning foot or spring
Needle: #90/14 sharp
Tension: top, loosened; bobbin, slightly loosened
Thread: gold metallic sewing thread, gold metallic ribbon thread or narrow decorative braid
Fabric: 1/4" (6mm) square scraps to match gold thread (cut out 2)
Accessories: permanent white opaque marker, 5" (13 cm) or 7" (18cm) spring hoop, glue stick, epoxy (2-tube type) or Goop
Stabilizer: water-soluble
Miscellaneous: small beads to match earrings, earring posts or clips

Prepare the hoop as before with two layers of water-soluble stabilizer.

6.11 *Draw two rectangle patterns on water-soluble stabilizer.*

Draw two small rectangles with the white opaque marker. Slip the hoop under the needle and dip the needle down to bring the ribbon to the top. Hold the ribbon to one side as you stitch around the perimeter of

6.12 *Stitch once around the perimeter of each of the rectangles.*

the rectangle and then over the ribbon at the starting point to anchor it. Clip off the end close to the stabilizer. Continue by stitching up and back to the left across the rectangle. Keep your rows close together. When you

6.13 *Stitch down and back in close rows, beginning at A and ending at B.*

reach the lower left corner, turn the hoop a quarter turn to the right and stitch up, down, and across the rectangle, perpendicular to the direction you first stitched. For the last pass, turn your hoop back a quarter turn.

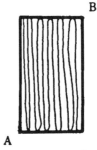

6.14 *Turn and stitch in rows perpendicular to the first pass, begining at B and ending at A.*

With the white marker, draw a line across slightly beyond the bottom of the earring to indicate how long you want the fringe to extend (I suggest 1/4" [6mm] to 3/8" [9.5mm]). Before you begin stitching the third and final pass, place a tiny scrap of matching fabric over the place where you'll glue the earring back later. (You are working with the underside of the earrings on top; the top, or ribbon side, is underneath.)

Stitch the last pass slowly. Again you'll stitch up and back as you did on the first layer, but instead of stitching to the bottom edge, stitch beyond to the fringe line you've drawn. Then

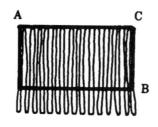

6.15 *Fringe earrings on the third pass by stitching from A to C.*

stitch back to the top as close as you can next to the first row without stitching on top of it. Continue to stitch across the rectangle. The last two rows are completed by stitching down and back to the top, leaving a 1/2" (13mm) tail of thread and ribbon to work in underneath later when you sew on the beads. Remove the stabilizer from the hoop, cut around the earrings, then hold them under a

faucet to wash out any remaining stabilizer. Place the earrings between two pieces of toweling and squeeze out the moisture. Leave the fringe in loops or clip the ends to fray the ribbon.

Pull the ribbon end to the underside and hold it there, catching it in the stitches as you attach the beads by hand.

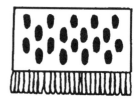

6.16 *Attach beads to the earrings by hand.*

Glue on the backings as described in the previous directions.

Project 34: Plaid earrings

The last earring style is a long triangle shape stitched with two layers of variegated machine-embroidery rayon. When completed, the stiffened, gauzelike, plaid earrings are manipulated into three-dimensional shapes.

Supplies needed:
Stitch width: 0
Stitch length: 0
Feed dogs: lowered or covered
Presser foot: darning foot or spring
Needle: #90/14 sharp
Tension: top, normal; bobbin, normal
Thread: rayon variegated machine-embroidery thread on top and thread of one color found in the variegated on the bobbin
Accessories: white opaque marker, 5" (13cm) or 7" (18cm) spring hoop
Stabilizer: water-soluble type
Miscellaneous: earring posts or clips, epoxy or Goop

Prepare the hoop as before and draw your pattern on two layers of water-soluble stabilizer.

6.17 *Pattern to trace onto water-soluble stabilizer*

Stitch up and back from the point to what will become the earring fringe. Stitch in the first

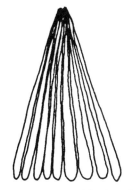

6.18 *Stitch up and back within the triangle.*

pass without crossing threads—if you can help it—but stitch the rows as close together as possible. When finished, go back across the earrings, traveling from the top point down to a place 1/4" (6mm) from the bottom fringed edge.

6.19 *Stitch across and back.*

Remove the stabilizer from the hoop, cut around the earrings, then run water over them to wash out some of the stabilizer. Leave enough residue in the earrings to stiffen them. Roll up from the pointed end and hold it in place with a pin, if necessary, until dry.

Use epoxy or Goop to glue backings on when the earring is completely dry.

Another idea? Make the same variegated earrings, but don't roll down the top. Instead, attach a hook finding for pierced ears or poke a plain, small ball post through the needle lace earrings.

Don't limit yourself; try other shapes and styles while experimenting with the many new threads and ribbons available today for machine embroidery (see Color Plate 8 and 14).

6.20 *Roll into three-dimensional earrings.*

Using buttons, bangles, and beads

Buttons are my decoration of choice for the following jewelry. Versatile decorations, they can be as beautiful as beads and often are interchangeable with them.

"Shell buttons were drilled with two holes, then sewn on to garments purely for decoration." Doesn't this sound like a reference to fashion today? It is—and also about fashion back in 2000 B.C., when buttons were first invented. Then they weren't used as closures at all—that use was dreamed up in the thirteenth century, when someone invented a buttonhole.

Once again, the hottest additions to clothes are decorative buttons—sewn to clothing, used as shoe clips, or decorating necklace tubes.

Project 35: Button earrings

6.21 *Decorated button earring*

When my mother wanted earrings for a new suit she'd purchased, I thought of buttons. She requested white and black, but jade was one of the colors in the jacket, so I thought I'd make a combination of colors for her (see Color Plate 4).

Supplies needed:

Buttons: 2 black-and-white buttons grooved in a grid pattern so black lines are visible beneath a white surface

Jewelry findings: several large jump rings, earring backings, two head pins

Beads: assorted sizes of white, black, and jade

Tools: needle-nosed pliers

Miscellaneous: Fray Check, Goop, several white sequins, 24" (61cm) white soutache braid, fine beading wire

To begin decorating the black-and-white earrings, I first opened a large silver jump ring with a needle-nosed pliers. I pushed this through and around the

6.22 *Open a large jump ring and place it around holes in the button.*

two buttonholes and pressed the ends together. Then for each earring I cut two 5" (13cm) lengths of white soutache. These I slipped through the jump ring, then pulled them through so they were doubled. I held the first one together with an overhand knot about 1" (2.5cm) from the jump ring, and another knot at the end. The other piece was lined up with the piece previously knotted, and the knot I tied in that one fell between those on the other piece of braid. I used Fray Check on the cut ends of the braid.

6.23 *Add two pieces of white soutache braid and knot them.*

I slipped several black-and-white beads on two jump rings, then attached them to braids above the knots.

Large (3mm) black beads were slipped onto a head pin, and that was attached to the center jump ring. Then I added a long, black, triangular

6.24 *String beads on jump rings and add above knots on braids.*

bead to the top of the black beaded head pin.

With fine beading wire, I strung a conglomeration of black, jade green, and white beads, and added a few white sequins as well, leaving enough wire at the top to bend into a loop later. After going through the last bead, I went back up through several beads

6.25 *Add beads to head pin, then add that and a long triangular bead to the center jump ring.*

again (starting at the bead next to the last), and cut off the end of the wire. Going back to the top, I bent the wire over the middle jump ring.

The earring is complete, except for the backing. Those I glued slightly above the centers of the buttons.

6.26 *String beads on to beading wire and bend one end of the wire over center jump ring. Run the other end of the wire up through several beads and clip off.*

Afterthought: You can make instant button earrings if you eliminate the decoration. Fabric stores offer everything from disks filled with rhinestones to Snoopy or Oreo cookies. All you have to do is remove the shank with a wire cutter (use for metal or plastic shanks), file the shank down flat if necessary, and glue on an earring backing (see Color Plates 1 and 10).

Instant Idea

1. Glue beautiful buttons to barrette blanks and then to findings.

Slip ornate shank buttons on to bobby pins for quick hair ornaments.

Old button jewelry

I've had a button collection for years. Oh, I didn't collect them on purpose. Instead, I was given both of my grandmas' button boxes, my mother-in-law's jar of buttons, and I was the highest bidder when an auctioneer once threw in a box of hundreds of buttons to "sweeten the pot," and all my relatives have given me their buttons instead of feeling guilty about tossing them out.

Once in awhile I looked through them, culled out those that looked interesting, and stored them according to color or type. On occasion my granddaughters dug through them and strung them on dental floss or elastic thread to make chunky necklaces.

I knew I should be doing something to display them, but I wasn't interested in sewing them to display boards. And when I used the unique ones on a garment, I always removed them again when the garment was beyond wearing.

I made earrings (as above) from some of them and can slip the top prong of a bobby pin through the shank, to make a hair ornament for one of the girls.

Last summer I found a crocheted button bracelet at a flea market, and since then I've been making button bracelets. Although my flea market find was crocheted with heavy elastic thread, I use a faster method. I buy 2"-

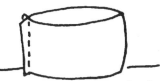

6.27 Use 2" (5cm) waistband elastic as a base for the button bracelet.

wide (5cm-wide) waistband elastic and join it so it fits comfortably on my wrist. Then I sew buttons to it with fine elastic thread so it stretches with the waistband elastic. The buttons are overlapped and sewn on to cover the edges of the elastic (see Color Plate 2) and no one sees the waistband elastic, and no one knows I didn't spend an hour crocheting (see Color Plate 10).

6.28 Stitch buttons on by hand with elastic thread.

Project 36:
Indian medicine necklace

6.29 *Indian medicine necklace*

A card on the necklace in the showcase at the Indian bead shop said: "Believed to impart to the wearer the powers of the spirits found within." I couldn't resist. No, it's not an authentic Indian artifact, but it's fun to imagine it is. I had to have it...whoa, it was over $200! As I continued to look at it, I realized (though I hate to admit it) I owned many of the things dangling from the strings of black beads, and I could buy the rest at the shop (that was the idea, right?) or substitute other things I had at home. I had to make one. This is not a twin to the one I saw, but I planned to hang this up as a wall decoration so I wasn't concerned that it grew too large and heavy to wear (see Color Plate 11).

The shop's necklace included brass, bone, and glass beads; an Indian head penny; a buffalo nickel; carved pipe stem; coyote fang; bobcat claws; bear, elk, and bovine teeth; brass thimble; deer antler and dew claws; ermine tail; rawhide medicine pouch; ivory scrimshaw; and arrowhead. Many, but not all, of the teeth and claws are plastic replicas.

Supplies needed:

Beads: three hanks 2mm black beads (I didn't use all of them), a dozen black beads of larger sizes, bonelike white plastic beads in pipe shapes, long box-shaped white ceramic beads, shell, copper, antler, clay, vegetable (see Chapter 2), wood, pony, two black (Sculpey III) spacers, seed beads in several colors, turquoise chips

Bangles: two brass thimbles, fishing swivels and snaps, arrow heads, deer dew claws, plastic bovine teeth, bells, metal cones, plastic scrimshaw

Cord: tiger tail, beading thread

Jewelry findings: two crimp beads, two jump rings, lobster claw clasp set

Tools: needle-nosed pliers, beading needle

Miscellaneous: 3" x 9" (8cm x 23cm) soft leather, strips of chamois and Ultrasuede in assorted colors, ermine tail, two arrow heads, feathers, bones

Usually I string necklaces on a cork board purchased originally for smocking. It works

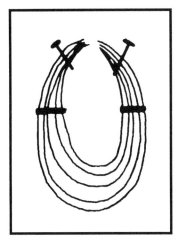

6.30 *Work on a cork board or ceiling tile to keep all five strands in place.*

beautifully (you can use ceiling tile, too). I strung my beads (I had five strands going at once) and pinned as I progressed. Each strand is a different length and I needed two spacer bars to

hold the threads apart evenly. Not knowing where to find two spacers that looked fitting, I made plain, black spacers with black Sculpey III clay (See Chapter 2).

6.31 *Make a Sculpey spacer.*

These spacer beads are made in a strip with five equally spaced, parallel holes. The five strands of beads are strung through the holes to keep them spaced evenly. The spacers are placed slightly lower than the collarbone when wearing the necklace. Measure their placement before you begin to string your beads.

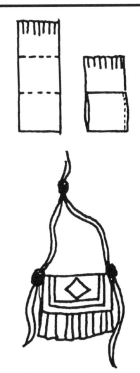

6.32 *Sew up a small, 3″ x 9″ (8cm x 23cm), beaded leather purse. A. Cut suede rectangle and and sew on seed beads. B. Fold up 1/3 at bottom and stitch sides together. Fringe flap. C. Attach a suede cord to purse, add beads, and attach it to the necklace.*

6.33 *Add coins, beads, teeth, claws, bells, etc.*

The closure was planned ahead of time, too, and I decided to use a thimble (also available at the shop) at each end. Then I attached jump rings and lobster claw clasps.

Often you see thimbles on Indian clothing—when dancing, the thimbles sound like tiny bells—so I thought it appropriate to use them. To poke a hole in the top of a thimble, I placed the thimble topside down on a piece of scrap lumber and hammered a long nail through the center top. Then I removed the nail and sanded the top smooth.

Black beads (2mm) hold it all together, and I incorporated black beads in several other sizes, too. I dug through a box of fur I have and stripped off long strands and glued them inside brass cones along with beads and suede strips. I stopped short of adding our children's baby teeth, though they may still find their place there (yes, I really do save everything).

Inventing things is more fun than buying them. Thanks to the Tomahawk River Fur Trading Company (see Sources of Supplies), I was inspired to make a magical wall decoration that provokes laughter and "wow's" by everyone who sees it—a real conversation piece. I love it.

Using casting resins, laminates, and acrylic sprays

Find pictures in magazines. Have them laminated at a print shop. You may want to use commemorative postage stamps, quilt patterns, marbleized paper, or your own drawings or paintings for a pin. Use colored photos of your kids, dog, needlepoint, whathave-you. Visit art galleries and museums to find postcards of favorite drawings or paintings. If adaptable to pins, trim pin areas to size and laminate them to preserve and wear them.

Another way to preserve artwork, postcards and photos is to use casting resins. Available at craft stores, the resin (usually you mix two thick liquids together) is poured over the picture and hardens. It gives your jewelry a thick (40 layers of varnish) plastic coat. Find a road map that shows your hometown or a vacation spot you love (see Color Plate 14). Cut out that area and glue it to cardboard. Make a pin or earrings by pouring casting resin over them. Pour it over colorful puzzle pieces and hang from earring findings. It's hard to run out of ideas (see Color Plates 3, 7, 13 and 16).

Use a spray acrylic to protect your paper jewelry if you don't want a heavy, plastic look.

Hint: To find the area in a picture you want to preserve, cut a square or circle (the size of the pin or earring you wish to make) out of the middle of a piece of black construction paper. Place the hole over the picture you're considering to find exactly that part you wish to use. Trace around the inside of the paper piece; then cut out the picture.

6.34 *Frame a design to make an earring.*

Following are more ideas for jewelry finished with casting resin, laminates, or spray acrylic:

Handmade paper jewelry

Handmade paper is a favorite of mine. Sometimes I make it myself, but it is also available through mail order or in art stores. The next jewelry idea was born when I visited one of our boys at school. We walked along the bluffs looking over the Mississippi River and I collected a handful of weeds and grasses. When I got home, I made paper from it and sent him a note inside.

One of my friends gathers flowers from the gardens of people she visits, dries them, and makes note cards from them for their Christmas gifts or writes a thank you note on them when she returns home from her visit.

Once I learned to make paper, I turned out reams of it. But what could I make with it other than note cards? I made earrings. If you use the weeds, flowers, and grasses from friends' yards, you can't find a more personalized gift. I even found a way of including a thank you (it could be a "Happy Birthday" just as easily) inside one earring design. Directions follow:

Project 37: Greeting card earrings

6.35 *Greeting card earring*

These earrings are both a greeting card and a gift (see Color Plate 12).

Supplies needed:

Paper: handmade or watercolor paper, small strip of writing paper

Findings: two jump rings, two french ear hooks

Miscellaneous: gold marker, ruler, pencil, circle cutter and mat or paper cutting scissors and compass

First I cut two circles from the blue handmade paper. To cut a perfect circle, I used a circle cutter. It works like a

6.36 *Circle cutters have adjustable ruler and blade.*

compass, with a pin at one side, a blade on the other side. Between the two is an adjustable ruler. Set the ruler for the radius (I used 1" [2.5cm] and cut slowly and carefully). The paper I chose has fine grasses in it so I took my time cutting to prevent tearing the paper. Decorative papers other than handmade are available, too. Watercolor paper works well, or visit an art or craft store to find art papers of different colors, weights, and textures.

After I cut the circle, I used a gold permanent marker to color the edge. The handmade paper is porous and the gold ink soaks in unevenly, creating a decorative, feathered edge.

Then, using the radius length and a compass, mark off six points around the edge of the circles (mark these lightly on what will be the inside of the card). Use a ruler

6.37 *Mark off six points on the circle.*

to make an equilateral triangle (and you thought you'd never use geometry) by connecting lines from three points. Score the lines as you draw them by pressing down on the pencil so that folding on the lines is easy.

Reinforce what will be the top point by cutting out a small scrap of the same paper and gluing it to the inside, where you will punch the hole for

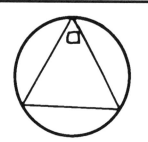

6.38 *Reinforce area at the top.*

the jump ring. Next, fold in the flaps as shown. Then write a message on a strip of paper, fold it up accordion style, and slip it into the card. Leave an end protruding so the recipient can pull it out to read her greeting.

6.39 *Fold in flaps and tuck in message.*

Use a darning needle to carefully poke a hole in the point. Slip in a jump ring and add a french ear hook.

Spray the earrings with a protective acrylic, or leave them as is to retain the natural, handmade look.

Project 38: Pentagon paper earrings

Cut handmade paper into 1/2"-wide (13mm-wide) strips, at least 4" (10cm) long for ease in knotting.

Color one side of the strips with a gold marker. Run the marker along the edge of the other side.

Tie each strip into an overhand knot, then tighten it down, flatten, and cut back to the pentagon for one pair. Leave protruding ends cut on a slant for the other pair. Glue backings on with Goop.

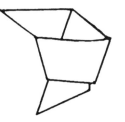

6.40 *Cut ends of the paper strip on slants for earrings.*

6.41 *Cut off ends of paper to create the five sides of a pentagon earring.*

Use casting resin to cover the surfaces if you wish, or spray with a coat of acrylic.

Afterthought: Use fabric instead of paper. Tie an overhand knot in a strip of fabric (first fold in the raw edges, then fold again if you don't want shaggy earrings). Poke the ends under the knot (clip off excess fabric) and glue to an earring post.

You may want to use a coating of glue or Stiffy for these, but I still think soft is better. Spray with Scotchgard for protection. It is invisible.

Commercial plastic and muslin pins

An alternative to laminating or using resins might be the round, clear plastic circle pins available in craft shops. The large, 3" (8cm) size may turn you off, however, and whatever you place inside must be thin, ruling out most embroidery and some fabrics. But if you use them, all you have to do is snap the front and back together with fabric or paper between the halves. Pins are already attached.

Badge-a-Minit is another way to preserve those works of art or pithy sayings. Like the plastic pins above, they have the same limitations. And plastic is always placed on top of the fabric or paper. Machines are available by mail order (see Sources of Supplies).

If you want fabric without a plastic cover, then use the largest covered button set (size 75), or make pins as described in Chapter 4.

Three-inch (7.6cm), muslin-covered pins are available at craft shops, too. Paint them with markers or glue things to them—or do both.

Visit the library for other jewelry ideas. Find three-dimensional flower ideas, origami designs, or holiday icons you can adapt to jewelry; then look through costume books and old Sears and Roebuck and Montgomery Wards catalogs for great inspirations.

Instant Ideas

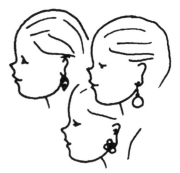

6. Keep children busy making earrings from Christmas ornaments, tiny pine cones, doll house miniatures, teeny pom poms (five for an earring or one large one), padded stars, and silk flowers (all available at craft shops).

2. Use clip earrings for pins (as per the 1930s and 1940s) at necklines or use them as scarf or shoe clips.

3. Use barrettes for scarf clips.

4. Decorate collar points with post earrings, or use them for small pins.

After Christmas, spray small crackers and cookies with acrylic and let children glue backings on for earrings.

(Optional: Dip small Christmas balls into glue, then glitter. Do the same with pine cones.)

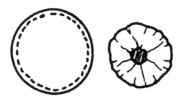

5. Make yoyo earrings with a circles of fabric-covered foam mounting board inside to hold them in place.

Cut up corrugated cardboard into small shapes, then let your children paint them with squiggles, stripes, and dots; glue and stack them into designs for pins and earrings. (They don't have to be the same to be a pair of earrings.)

7. Two related, small pins? String a chain between them for a new look.

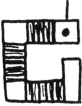

10. Wrap hoop earrings with strips of silk to match a blouse.

8. Stitch or serge fine wire to a pocket handkerchief. Insert into the pocket and arrange the top decoratively.

9. Know a telephone repairman? Beg colorful wire from him and make earrings or bracelets. Slip beads into a tube and wrap between them with telephone wire.

11. Find those 1960s pins at thrift shops and wear them on hats, headbands, or a black velvet cord.

Afterword

"Serendipity—the faculty for making desirable discoveries by accident."

"Serendipity" would be a fitting title for this book. When I began making jewelry, I was bombarded by desirable accidental discoveries. They came from friends ("That reminds me of—") and from my own memory, as well as notebooks I keep.

My brain has always adapted everything I see to needlework. Now it skips on to jewelry automatically. One idea always makes me think of another, which leads me to another, and I simply can't run out of serendipitous ideas.

I want you to be inspired to do the same. I showed you the basics. Now you can duplicate the jewelry I made, or you can take them all a step further and off in new directions.

I know what joy comes from working with fibers, making original gifts, spending time making things with your children or grandchildren, turning on your creativity. Try it; you'll love it, too.

Sources of Supplies

Atlanta Thread and Supply Co.
695 Red Oak Rd.
Stockbridge, GA 30281

  Thread, sewing supplies, buttons

Badge-A-Minit
Box 800
LaSalle, IL 61301

  Badge pin machines and supplies

Beadworks
139 Washington St.
South Norwalk, CT 06854

  Clasps, pins, findings, threads, beads

The Bee Lee Co.
PO Box 36108
Dallas Texas 75235-1108

  Sewing supplies, buttons, rick-rack,
ribbon

Berman Leathercraft
145 South St.
Boston, MA 02111

  Leather

Bovis Bead Co.
PO Box 111
Bisbee, AZ 85603

  Trade beads of the world

Boycan's Craft and Art Supplies
PO Box 897
Sharon, PA 16146

The Button Shop
PO Box 1065
Oak Park, IL 60304

  Buttons, rick-rack, presser feet

Clotilde, Inc.
Box 22312
Ft. Lauderdale, FL 33335

  Presser feet, notions, rotary cutters, mats

Craft Gallery
PO Box 145
Swampscott, MA 01907

  Needlework and craft supplies

Field's Fabrics
1695-44th St., S.E.
Grand Rapids, MI 49508

  Ultrasuede, Facile, Caress, UltraLeather
Samples $10

The Garden of Beadin'
PO Box 1535
Redway, CA 95560

  Beads

Gem-o-rama, Inc.
150 Recreation Park Dr. Bay #8
Hingham, MA 02043

  Beads

Home-Sew
Bethlehem, PA 18018

  Lace, rick-rack, buttons
$.25 catalog

KUMAco
 PO Box 3363
Peabody, MA 01960

  Beads

Mini-Magic
3675 Reed Rd.
Columbus, OH 43220

  Fine ribbons, fabrics, thread, lace, trims

Nancy's Notions
333 Beichl Ave.
Beaver Dam, WI 53916

Presser feet, notions, rotary cutters, mats

Newark Dressmaker Supply
6473 Rock Rd. PO Box 2448
Lehigh Valley, PA 18001

Thread

Ornamental Resources
Box 3010
1427 Miner St.
Idaho Springs, CO 80452

Loose-leaf notebook catalog $15. Updated through the year. This is a goldmine.

The Perfect Notion
566 Hoyt St.
Darien, CT 06820

Sewing supplies

Promenade Enterprises, Inc.
PO Box 2092
Boulder, Colorado 80306

Beads and beading supplies

Quilters' Resource, Inc.
PO Box 148850
Chicago, IL 60614

Lamés, old buttons, braids, trinkets, Quick Crafter for bow and fringe making

Salem Industries, Inc.
PO Box 43027
Atlanta, GA 30336

Olfa cutters, rulers

Sax Arts and Crafts
PO Box 51710
New Berlin, WI 53151

Art supplies, jewelry kits, Craft Beader, handmade paper

Sew Fit Co.
PO Box 565
LaGrange IL, 60526

Rotary cutters, mats, presser feet

Sewing Emporium
1087 Third Avenue
Chula Vista, CA 92010

Sewing accessories and presser feet

Solar-Kist Corp.
PO Box 273
LaGrange, IL 60525

Teflon pressing sheet

Sulky of America
3112 Broadpoint Dr.
Harbor Heights, FL 33983

Rayon machine embroidery thread

Susan of Newport
Box 3107
Newport Beach, CA 92663

Ribbons and laces

Tandy Leather Co.
PO Box 791
Ft. Worth, TX 76101

Leather, leather punch, beads

Tomahawk River Fur Trading Co.
Old Depot Highway 51
Minocqua, WI 54548

No catalog, but will send out orders. Phone: (715) 356- 2736. This is where I saw the medicine necklace.

TSI, Inc.
101 Nickerson St.
PO Box 9266
Seattle, WA

Beads, Fimo, jewelry tools, findings

Western Trading Post
PO Box 9070
Denver, CO 80209-0070

Beads, porcupine quills, fur. Catalog $3.00

Magazines

Write for rates.

Aardvark Territorial Enterprise
PO Box 2449
Livermore, CA 94550

Newspaper jammed with all kinds of information about all kinds of embroidery, design, and things to order. They have beads, feathers, cords, and rayon machine embroidery threads.

Fiberarts
50 College St.
Asheville, NC 28801

Gallery of the best fiber artists, including those who work in machine stitchery.

Ornament Magazine
PO Box 2349 San Marcos,
CA 92079-9806

Wearables and jewelry design at their best

Sew News
PO Box 1790
Peoria, IL 61656

Monthly tabloid, mostly about garment sewing

Surface Design Journal
4111 Lincoln Blvd., Suite 426
Marina del Rey, CA 90292

Threads
Box 355
Newton, CT 06470

Magazine on all fiber crafts

Treadleart
25834 Narbonne Ave., Ste. 1
Lomita, CA 90717

Bimonthly about machine embroidery. Catalog, too.

Bibliography

The Art and Craft of Ribbonwork, Body Blueprints.

Ashley, Clifford W. *The Ashley Book of Knots.* Doubleday & Co., 1944.

Blakelock, Virginia L. *Those Bad, Bad Beads.* Blakelock, 1988.

Carey, Margret. *Beads and Beadwork of East and South Africa.* Shire Ethnography, 1986.

Campbell-Harding, Valerie and Pamela Watts. *Machine Embroidery: Stitch Techniques.* Batsford, 1989.

Champion. *The Basics of Bead Stringing.* Borjay, 1985.

Clucas, Joy. *The New Machine Embroidery.* David and Charles, 1987.

Conaway, Judith. *Soft Jewely.* Simon & Schuster, 1978.

Dormer, Peter and Ralph Turner. *The New Jewelry.* Thames and Hudson, 1985.

Editors of Sunset books. *Jewelry You Can Make.* Lane Publishing Co., 1975.

Editors of Sunset Books. *Stitchery.* Lane Publishing Co., 1974.

Enthoven, Jacqueline. *The Stitches of Creative Embroidery.* Reinhold Book Corp., 1964.

Glassman, Judith. *Step by Step Beadcraft.* Golden Press, 1974.

Hofler, Robert and Cyn. Zarco. *Wild Style.* Simon & Schuster, 1985.

Holz, Loretta. *The How-To Book of International Dolls.* Crown Publishers, 1980.

Howell-Koehler, Nancy. *Soft Jewelry Design, Techniques, Materials.* Davis, 1976.

Kliot, Jules and Kaethe. *Bead Work.* Lacis, 1984.

Lane, Maggie. *Maggie Lane's Book of Beads.* Scribner's Sons, 1979.

Lavitt, Wendy. *American Folk Dolls.* Alfred A. Knopf, 1982.

Lyford, Carrie A. *Quill and Beadwork of the Western Sioux.* R. Schneider, Publishers, 1983.

Miller, Harrice Simons. *Costume Jewelry.* House of Collectibles, 1990.

Mulari, Mary. *Accents for Your Style.* Mary's Productions, 1990.

Mulvagh, Jane. *Costume Jewelry in Vogue.* Thames and Hudson, 1988.

Old-Fashioned Ribbon Art. Ribbon Art Publishing Co. Reprint Dover Publications, 1986.

The Ribbon Art Book. Vols.1-3. Ribbon Art Publishing Co., 1923.

Shannon, Faith. *Paper Pleasures.* Weidenfeld & Nicolson, 1987.

Solberg, Ramona. *Inventive Jewelry-making.* Van Nostrand Reinhold, 1972.

Spears, Therese. *Beaded Clothing Techniques.* Promenade Publishing, 1984.

Thompson, Angela. *Embroidery with Beads.* Batsford, 1974.

Tomalin, Stefany. *Beads!* David and Charles, 1988.

Index

twisted satin stitches, 39-40
worry doll necklace, 41-43
rick-rack, 56-58
as supplies for soft jewelry, 3
threads covering, 35-38
threads and fabric, manipulating, 49
tubes from collars, 48-49
Cornstarch beads, 14
Couching, 32
Craft Beader, 4
Crimp beads, 5-6, 59-60
Crochet hook, 5

Denim earrings, 19
Denim necklace, wrapped and wound, 17-18
Doll pins, 88-91

E-6000 jewelry adhesive, 3
Earrings
  button, 113-114
  and button covers, 95-96
  clips for, 5
  denim, 19
  fishing fly, 84
  french ear hooks for, 5
  gold braid rectangles, 109-110
  gold triangle, 107-108
  greeting card, 121-122
  kidney wires for, 5
  lace, 105
  pentagon paper, 122
  plaid, 111-112
  posts for, 5
  rick-rack, 97
  scraps and lace, 106
  thread, 106

Elna's net curtain foot, 2
Eye pins, 5, 60-61, 62

Fabric beads
  sewing, 22-25
  wrapping and winding, 16
Fabric Cord, 44, 50
Fabrics
  around beads, 16
  paints for, 5
  as supplies for soft jewelry, 3
Fasturn tube turners, 3
Feather hat ornament, 82-83
Feather lapel pin, 81
Feather ornaments, 80
Fiber cords, 60
Fiberfill, 3
Filled tubes, cords from, 44-45
Fisherman's knot, 65
Fishing fly earrings, 84
Fishing line, 36-38
527 jewelry cement, 3
Flower barrette, quilted and beaded, 29-31
Fluffy boa wrap, 76-78
Fray Check, 3, 21
Freezer paper, 3
French ear hooks, 5
Fringe forks, 3

General purpose foot, 2
Glass beads, 25
Glues, 3
Gold and pearls stick pin, 43
Gold braid rectangles, 109-110
Gold triangle earrings, 107-108
Goop, 3, 80
Greeting card earrings, 121-122
Griese's (Audrey) serged cords, 38

Handmade paper, 5, 120
Handmade paper jewelry, 120
Head pins, 5
Heart barrettes, 99-100
Heart pins, 99-100
Hemostat, 4
Hook and figure-8 eye, 6
Hooks, 4, 64
Household Goop, 3, 80

Idiot cord, 54-56
Indian doll pin, 90-91
Indian medicine necklace, 116-118
Instant ideas
  for beads, 13, 14, 16, 21, 25, 34
  for clasps and closures, 62, 64, 65
  for cords, 38, 40, 45, 46, 49
  for soft cores and hard surfaces, 114, 124-125
  for soft surfaces, 83, 86, 96, 99, 103

Jewelry. See Soft jewelry; specific types of
Jump rings, 5

Kidney wires, 5
Knitting machine, 1
Knitting needles, 1
Knots, 45, 62

Lace earrings, 105
Laminates, 119
Leather punch sets, 4
Lobster claw clasp set, 5, 59
Loop closure, 71